# Africa and the Afro-American Experience

# Africa and the Afro-American Experience

*Eight Essays*

edited by

LORRAINE A. WILLIAMS

 HOWARD UNIVERSITY PRESS • WASHINGTON, D.C. 1981

Printed in the United States of America

**Library of Congress Cataloging in Publication Data**
Main entry under title:

Africa and the Afro-American experience.

"A compilation of eight essays published in the Second series of historical publications of the Department of History at Howard University
between April 1, 1971, and May 1, 1973."
Includes index.
CONTENTS: Hansberry, W. L. Africana at Nsukka.—Brown, C. F.
The conversion experience in Axum during the fourth and fifth centuries.
[etc.] p.
1. Negroes—History—Addresses, essays, lectures. 2. Negroes—Biography. 3. Africa—History—Addresses, essays, lectures. I. Williams, Lorraine
A., comp. II. Howard University, Washington, D.C. Dept. of History.
Second series of historical publications.

E185.A25   1975        909′.04′96        74-34584

Hardcover ISBN 0-88258-030-2
Paperback ISBN 0-88258-087-6

Grateful acknowledgment is made to John W. Blassingame and Oxford
University Press for permission to reprint "Sambos and Rebels: The Char-
acter of the Southern Slave" from *The Slave Community* by John W.
Blassingame. Copyright © 1972 by Oxford University Press, Inc.

# Preface

The struggle of Black men and women in the United States for freedom is an exciting chapter in the history of mankind. Presently there is a special focus on Black history and on the role that Black people have played in the historical process in various parts of the world. Benjamin A. Quarles, in his essay "Black History's Diversified Clientele," emphasizes the diversified clientele of this significant aspect of history that has either been ignored or misrepresented until recently by most historians of the Western world. Black history's diversified clientele includes "the Black rank and file, the Black academicians, the Black revolutionary nationalists, and the white world, both scholarly and lay," according to Professor Quarles.

Black historians have a special responsibility to reassess and interpret the past that includes the historical and political linkages of Africans and Afro-Americans. Several of the essays presented here relate to these linkages. William Leo Hansberry, a pioneer in the study of ancient and medieval African history, reminded Howard University and other members of the academic community as early as 1922 that the study of African history presented a supreme opportunity to emphasize one of the most significant aspects of history. His essay, "Africana at Nsukka," is well grounded in this approach. Clifton F. Brown, a young scholar of Ethiopian history, is a disciple of William Leo Hansberry. Brown in his essay, "The Conversion Experience in Axum during the Fourth and Fifth Centuries," contributes information on a subject that has not been sufficiently studied. George Washington Williams, one of the earlier Black historians, was intellectually curious about the African heritage. In the essay "George Washington Williams and Africa," Professor John Hope Franklin presents a vivid account of Williams' impressions of Africa during a visit in 1890: "After extensive travel and an exploratory expedition in the Congo, he was shocked by the destructive impact of European imperialism." Alexander Crummell, another Black intellectual of the nineteenth century, believed that "the destiny of Blacks everywhere was tied to their fate anywhere." He was convinced of this as he traveled in Liberia and other parts of Africa, according to Otey M. Scruggs' essay, "We the Children of Africa in This Land: Alexander Crummell." Another essay that focuses attention on political developments in Africa is "Prelude to Disaster: An Analysis of the Racial Policies of Boer and British Settlers in South Africa before 1910," by Professor Okon Edet Uya.

This book also includes essays that emphasize different aspects of historical events in the United States and outstanding personalities who have contributed to the Black experience. The distinguished historian Rayford W. Logan presents a comparison of the personalities and contributions of "Two Bronze Titans: Frederick Douglass and William Edward Burghardt Du Bois," and John W. Blassingame presents a fresh approach to the character of the Southern slave by using slave narratives.

In the concluding essay, Benjamin A. Quarles reminds us that "in its work of restoring history's lost boundaries, the Black history of today is establishing new contacts and finding a new soul." This book is presented as an expression of that belief.

This publication, *Africa and the Afro-American Experience*, is a compilation of eight essays published in the Second Series of Historical Publications of the Department of History at Howard University between April 1, 1971, and May 1, 1973.

Lorraine A. Williams
Vice President
  for Academic Affairs
Howard University

May 1977

# Contents

# Africa
# and the
# Afro-American
# Experience

# I. Africana at Nsukka

## Some Distinctive Aspects of the Program of African Studies at the University of Nigeria

by William Leo Hansberry

### THE LOCALE

Nsukka is an ordinary Nigerian village in most respects, but the climate and the natural beauty of its immediate surroundings are of a character which unwary strangers from afar, on their initial visit, usually witness with profound surprise. Although it is situated in the midst of tropical Africa, the temperature at Nsukka, because of its high altitude, is prevailingly mild and pleasant throughout the year. As is generally true in the "lands of eternal spring" on the vast East African plateau, sweltering summers, comparable to those of many countries in the misnamed Temperate Zones, never occur; and the grim realities of northern winters are, of course, wholly unknown.

To most peoples in Western lands, tropical Africa is generally pictured as a vast and forbidding jungle filled with snorting elephants, roaring lions, and other bellowing beasts of disturbing mien; but the plant and animal life of the region about Nsukka is decidedly at odds with such preconceived notions. No elephants or lions or other jungle behemoths are to be found, except in an occasional zoo here and there, within hundreds of miles of Nsukka. It is an open country of great natural beauty which surrounds the village on every side. Grass-covered vales and dales and rolling hills of emerald green dominate the landscape as far as the eye can reach, and graceful palms and other flowering or fruit-bearing trees and shrubs dot the parklike scene in all directions. In other words, Nsukka is blessed by nature, as are the French and Italian Rivieras and parts of Florida and California, with what has been aptly described as "a millionaire's climate." Its natural surroundings recall the idyllic scenes attributed by the classical poets to the "Isles of the Blest."

## THE ACADEMIC CONTEXT

But Nsukka's natural beauty and natural advantages are not the things for which this little village is destined, in due course, to be most widely renowned. It is rather the fact that in its midst stands the University of Nigeria that will eventually bring to Nsukka its greatest acclaim. For the University of Nigeria, though one of the world's youngest, is nonetheless one of the world's most remarkable institutions of learning; and there are already many internal indications that it will grow in uniqueness and distinction with the passing of the years.

In January 1960 the beautiful site on which the university now stands was still covered by virgin growth which had dominated the landscape for countless decades. But in January 1963—a bare three years later—there stood on the same site a total of nearly 200 completed academic buildings and residential halls which had been erected at a cost of over $20,000,000. These buildings were occupied by nearly 2,000 students, enrolled in six different colleges,

and over 400 persons comprising the university's teaching
and administrative staffs and members of their immediate
families. All of the buildings mentioned were situated along
well-laid-out streets, and there was also in operation a large
power plant which provided the university with its own
electricity and water supply. On the edge of the main
campus there was a concrete stadium, much of it covered,
which was capable of seating over 20,000 persons.

Few, if any, university plants of comparable size in
Africa or elsewhere have ever been brought into being
quite so quickly; and nowhere, perhaps, have as many students of college level, and so many well-trained faculty
members—42 per cent of them with Ph.D. degrees—been
assembled in so short a period. On being asked on one occasion how it all happened, the Honorable Nnamdi Azikiwe,
the guiding genius of this remarkable undertaking, replied,
"It has been said that it is a miracle and I guess it is, but
be that as it may, I thank God for it."

The magiclike speed with which the University of
Nigeria was established is not, however, the most remarkable fact to be associated with its existence. Its uniqueness
resides, rather, in the purposes which it was designed to
serve and the deftness with which these purposes are
being carried out. One of its most immediate purposes, as
its name indicates, is to train Nigerians to serve Nigeria in
ways that will render the greatest good to the greatest
number of persons comprising the total Nigerian community. The university's most distinctive objective—as has
often been stated or implied by its founding fathers—is to
serve humanity at large by making it possible for mankind
in general, and Africans in particular, to see Africa whole
and true from an African point of view.

There is nothing about these grand objectives which
lies beyond the reach of practical accomplishment; but

their attainment will be, admittedly, no easy task. The responsible spokesmen for the university have made it clear on various occasions that they are thoroughly aware of the obstacles which lie athwart the pathways to these envisioned goals. They have repeatedly indicated or implied that while all of the colleges and departments of the university were established, and are being administered, with Nigeria's specific needs primarily in mind, this does not mean, as has been made quite clear, that the university's management was not thoroughly conscious of, and deeply concerned with, the larger role which the institution is capable of playing on the broad stage of world affairs. For it is true that from the beginning it was the plan of those who called this remarkable institution into being that the University of Nigeria could and should take the lead in uprooting and eradicating certain long-established and widely held misconceptions about Africa and its people which have beclouded, altogether too long, the real truth and the whole story about the nature of the total human environment and the history of the human race.

With this goal in mind, the founding fathers of the university, at the very start of their deliberations concerning academic objectives, proposed that a college of African studies should be established as soon as practicable. On December 15, 1961, or scarcely two years after ground was broken for the earliest of the university's buildings, the first step was taken to implement that proposal. On that occasion those in charge of planning and administration at the university did me the very signal honor—one for which I shall be ever grateful—of bestowing my name upon the projected college of African studies; and our purpose here today is to launch this fledgling institution on what, may we all hope, will be its triumphant way. Nothing, perhaps, is of greater moment at this stage in the development of the college of African studies than a clear assessment of its academic potentialities and a frank appraisal of the educational needs and the social ends that it should endeavor to serve. It is hardly necessary to say that neither of these undertakings is a simple task; but on such an occasion as this, one may be pardoned, perhaps, for making at least token gestures in these directions.

## OBJECTIVES AND POTENTIALITIES

If I have read aright the motives and objectives of those who were primarily responsible for the establishment of the college, it is my opinion that it was their hope and intention that the proposed program of African studies at Nsukka would be both quite broad and inclusive, yet rather distinctive in certain respects. Although the projected curriculum of the college would, in due course, embrace intensive studies of all the major facets of African life, its main concern in the immediate future would be with those geographic and historical aspects of the African story which up to now education at large, and most African studies programs in particular, have tended to ignore, or distort, or suppress.

As a consequence of such practices and attitudes, laypersons have been traduced by predatory outsiders into believing, for ulterior reasons, that Africa, in terms of human needs, is not only the poorest and the least desirable of the continents, but is now and always has been occupied by the least capable and the most backward of all the divisions of the human family. There is now and long has been available an abundance of well-authenticated geographic and historical evidence that makes it patently clear that all such concepts are hardly more than baseless stereotypes which have been foisted upon an unwary world by uninformed or malicious detractors for selfish and unholy ends.

Although these warped and debased concepts of Africa and its peoples are at odds with an abundance of reliable evidence which has been for the most part deliberately or inadvertently overlooked, it is nevertheless unfortunately true that much of this evidence—along with its geographic and historical import—is now and always has been rather inaccessible, for several reasons, to the world at large. This has grown out of the fact that a great deal of this evidence, though in itself of considerable antiquity, was first brought to light in modern times by investigators who were not only specialists in their various branches of geographic and anti-quarian research, but who reported their findings in the often highly technical and widely scattered publications of the many specialized branches of knowledge with which they were particularly concerned.

The findings relating to the nature of Africa's physical environment have been ferreted out and reported in the main by specialists working in the fields of geography, geology, climatology, mineralogy, ecology, and the soil sciences; while much of the most crucial evidence bearing upon the history and cultures of Africa and its peoples in earlier times has been discovered and recorded by specialists in the fields of archaeology, anthropology, paleontology, Oriental studies, classical literature, and related branches of antiquarian and historical research.

Here it should be pointed out that most of those who have been engaged in these various types of scientific or historical research in—or about—Africa have been motivated in the main either by disinterested intellectual curiosity or by quests for knowledge that would contribute to the economic or political advantages of themselves or to non-African agencies or nations that had sponsored their inquiries in one way or another. With rare exceptions, the economic, political, and social implications of their findings, so far as Africa's indigenous peoples were concerned, were matters of little if any moment to those by whom these investigations were carried out.

For these, and other reasons which will not be mentioned here, very few attempts were made during the period when most of Africa was under alien rule to assemble, coordinate, synthesize, and publicize in popular form the then abundantly available, but widely scattered and technically reported, facts about Africa's great natural wealth and the positive role its peoples had played in the grand epic of mankind's storied and unstoried past. As a consequence, most of these facts remained inaccessible to, and their import hidden from, the general public for many decades. The result was that Africa continued to be almost universally regarded as the devil's favorite playground and Clio's disinherited stepchild among the continents.

In planning the program for the college of African studies at Nsukka, this lag in the dissemination of the now available facts about the history and geography of Africa should not, in itself, influence necessarily the content of its curriculum. If the college serves the purposes which its founders had in mind, however, its teachers, students, and graduates will surely do much in due course to close this blighting gap in public knowledge of Africa's matchless wealth and ageless past, as masters of those specialized disciplines and techniques by which such knowledge has been acquired. With such training, the graduates of the college could become not only top-ranking African specialists and independent investigators in their own right, but masterful teachers who could convey effectively the essential facts of the long distorted African story to their uninformed fellow men who would have neither the time nor the training to ferret out such facts for themselves. In this way the traditionally maligned and misnamed Dark Continent could be—in the paraphrased words of the university's great chancellor—transformed almost overnight into "a continent of light."

### AFRICANA AND NATURE'S AFRICA

The time available to me in this inaugural address will permit only a very brief review of the character and import of the evidence which is making it necessary to revise fundamentally older concepts concerning Africa's natural advantages when compared with those of the other continents. Most of the information which is necessitating these revisions in older points of view is of comparatively recent acquisition. It is true that during the greater part of the last century, Africa, when judged on the strength of its natural capacity to meet basic human needs, was widely regarded by the ablest geographers of the age as the poorest and the most unpropitious of all the great land masses of the earth. Asia was then generally assumed to be not only the largest, the richest, and the most fertile of all the continents, but was credited with sharing with the Temperate Zone portions of Europe and the Americas most of the climatic and natural conditions that are most conducive to human development and human progress.

Most of these views, when first advanced, were based on historical inferences and geographic and climatic speculations but little else; for at that time the geographers of the Western world knew very little about the vast inland areas of either Africa or Asia. By the first decade of the present century, knowledge of the interior of both Asia and Africa had increased to such an extent as to indicate that earlier notions about nature's gifts to the two continents were hardly in accord with the geographic facts.

Writing in 1905, Meredith Townsend, a well-informed student of such matters, could assert that "Africa is probably more fertile and almost certainly richer than Asia"; and in 1908 Sir Harry H. Johnston, the great explorer, naturalist, and comparative geographer—and one who was credited with knowing more at first hand about Africa than any man of the age—startled most of his contemporaries by declaring, in effect, that the climate of most of tropical Africa, owing to its great altitude, "is generally agreeable and more equable" than that of tropical Asia. But of even greater surprise to most of his contemporaries was a published declaration by Sir Harry in which he announced that Africa was, in his opinion, "the richest continent in the world."

During the years that have passed since these then decidedly unorthodox appraisals of "Africa Tenebrosa" were first expressed, a vast amount of additional information of a comparative character has been assembled concerning the climate, the physical environment, and the natural resources of the several continents. This additional information has, on the whole, not only amplified and strengthened the evidence which led Sir Harry Johnston to conclude that Africa was the richest continent in the world, but has tended to demonstrate that Africa has been blessed with more of the major gifts of nature that are of primary use to man than has any of the other great land masses of the earth. In other words, an objective appraisal of all the relevant evidence would seem to indicate that Africa, despite its many limitations, is at once nature's most favored and mankind's most propitious continent. Let us look briefly at some of the more significant considerations upon which this rather untraditional appraisal is based.

As has been pointed out elsewhere, none of nature's gifts to man are more indispensable than land, water—particularly fresh water—sunlight or solar energy, and air. No one of these without the other three is, however, of much, if any, use to man; but land, water, sunlight, and air *in adequate amounts and in effective combinations* are nature's greatest gifts to human kind. Although air under most natural conditions is free and available in unlimited amounts everywhere on the globe, Nature has distributed her other three major gifts over the face of the earth in a rather uneven manner. She has been particularly partial in the manner in which she distributed land, water, and sunlight in effective combinations among the several continents.

Recent ecological investigations have shown that most forms of plant and animal life that are basic to human needs thrive best in those parts of the earth where the rainfall—or its equivalent in moisture brought in from the outside by irrigation—*averages* not less than 20 inches per annum, and where the climate, as expressed in temperature, averages not less than 90 to 120 consecutive frost-free days each year. These same investigations have shown that when moisture is adequate the so-called warm season crops such as sugarcane, cotton, coffee, cocoa, rubber, rice, peanuts, bananas, citrus fruits, pineapples, and most plants producing edible vegetable oils grow best in temperatures ranging from 64.8 to 98.6 degrees Fahrenheit during the growing season. Even the so-called cool season crops such as wheat, barley, oats, rye, and most Temperate Zone garden crops thrive best, if moisture is adequate, when and where the temperature ranges between 60 and 87.8 degrees Fahrenheit.

If space permitted, it could be abundantly demonstrated by relevant data drawn from every major area of the earth that in no part of the world are the rainfall requirements and the temperature ranges—technically known as the optimum growth temperatures—for both warm and cool season crops more consistently maintained over so large an area than in the great African continent. In this same connection it may also be pointed out that on the basis of recent and extensive investigations, climatologists are now generally agreed that for the great majority of mankind—including most of the inhabitants of the so-called Temperate Zones—human comfort and human health, so far as climate per se is concerned, are maintained under most conditions in temperatures ranging between 66 and 82 degrees Fahrenheit. Comparative studies of temperatures in all parts of the world have shown that in no continent are temperatures ranging between 66 and 82 degrees Fahrenheit more consistently maintained over as large an area as in tropical Africa.

Increasing discoveries concerning Africa's plutonium treasures have been of hardly less revolutionary import than were the unexpected revelations concerning the optimum climatic conditions in so much of the continent. Field surveys in recent decades have revealed that Nature has bestowed her mineral wealth on the African continent with an exceptionally generous hand. In the light of evidence now available it would appear that Africa has the world's largest known reserves of diamonds, gold, cobalt, columbite, vanadium, vermiculite, tantalum, beryllium, and phosphate rock; and although the evidence is, as of now, somewhat less certain, it would appear that the same is probably true for uranium, copper, manganese, high-grade bauxite, the platinum metals, asbestos, and high-grade iron ores. Recent discoveries in Uganda, the Katanga, and elsewhere have tended to indicate that tin and lithium—the lightest of metals—should be added to the latter list.

Of considerable significance in this same connection is the fact that recent surveys have revealed that tropical

Africa is potentially capable of producing vast quantities of hydroelectric power by which many of Africa's minerals could be most effectively processed. For it is true that although Africa—when the desert and semidesert regions are excluded—constitutes only about one-fifth of the earth's land surface, it possesses nevertheless, according to latest estimates, about 42 per cent of the world's potential hydroelectric power. This is nearly twice as much as Asia's potential and substantially more than that of North America, Europe, Australia, and South America combined.

Here it may be noted in passing that in 1948 what was then known as French Equatorial Africa and the French Cameroons combined were estimated to have more potential hydroelectric power than Canada, Mexico, and the United States put together; while that of the Belgian Congo, with Ruanda-Urundi added, exceeded the combined total for China, the USSR in Asia, India, and Pakistan. According to the same estimates, Ethiopia's potential was approximately equal to that of France, and the same was true of Liberia; while the horsepower potential of Nigeria and the British Cameroons exceeds that of France, Germany, and Britain combined.

By exploiting effectively these vast reserves of potential hydroelectric power, which are generally located in close proximity to vast mineral and forest reserves, it will be possible to develop in tropical Africa a whole series of electrometallurgical and electrochemical industries which could specialize in the processing of aluminum, manganese, ferrosilicon, phosphorus, silicon carbide, magnesium, wood pulp, and a host of other mineral and vegetable products which could serve well not only Africa's needs but the needs of the world at large.

It was, no doubt, just such facts as have been here passed in hurried review that the late Carveth Wells—a distinguished English publicist—had in mind when he summed up some years ago his estimate of the very important part Africa's natural wealth would play in the world of the future. Writing in this connection, he observes that "with her vast resources, both developed and undeveloped, there is every reason to expect Africa to become an industrial continent able not only to build great industries almost entirely upon her own resources, but to become as well the greatest exporter of raw materials in the world."

This statement by Carveth Wells, together with the other geographic considerations in the paragraph which preceded it, may be taken as a kind of overview of one of the distinctive aspects of the curriculum which the college of African studies at Nsukka proposes to develop in intensive detail in the near future. Another distinctive aspect of the college's program, to which even greater attention will be given, will be that part of the curriculum which will be concerned with giving all interested students a thorough-going acquaintance with that vast body of historical materials which are now available for the study of Africa's pre-colonial past—that is to say, during the ages when the African was master in his own house.

## *OVERVIEW OF AFRICANA ANTIQUA AT NSUKKA*

Contrary to what is generally supposed, reliable historical materials treating of, or relating to, early civilizations in tropical Africa are, when collectively considered, exceptionally abundant; but, as has been previously remarked, they are seldom as conveniently accessible as could be desired. They include all the types of historical materials that are customarily employed by those who have chosen for themselves the engrossing task of endeavoring to reconstruct mankind's storied and unstoried past; and they date from the present age back to the most remote epochs of human time. Some of these historical materials are represented by written records, monumental remains, and other relics of the past which were discovered or rediscovered many years ago, but others have been only very recently brought to light. In a number of instances these discoveries were the results of carefully planned and systematically directed efforts, but many were accidental and unsought but highly welcomed fruits of beneficent chance.

Africa has been, of course, the scene of most of these discoveries, but some of them were made in Europe and Asia, indeed, in regions as far afield as the island lands of the Indian Ocean and the South Seas. Many of these historical materials were of a character which neither those who first brought them to light nor any one else had much reason to expect; some have been, in fact, of such a nature as to cause profound surprise.

Perhaps the least expected or most surprising of these materials are those dating from what historians are wont to call Stone Age times, or the Age of Prehistoric Man. To understand how great has been this surprise, it is necessary to point out that as late as 1910 it was generally believed in academic circles that Africa had played but a very minor role in the early history of the human race. Although mankind was known to have existed on earth for hundreds of thousands of years, the evidence available in 1910 was so limited that it was then commonly supposed that most of Africa had been almost without human inhabitants during the greater part of that period.

In keeping with the then widely accepted hypothesis that Asia was the birthplace of man and the cradleland of civilization, most students of human origins were of the opinion that all of the earliest peoples and cultures of Africa had entered that continent from Asia, and that for tens of thousands of years these had been confined for the most part to the coastal region lying along the southern shore of the Mediterranean Sea. The rest of Africa, it was believed, had not been colonized by human beings until toward the very end of the Stone Age. Most students of the matter thought that this did not occur until about ten or fifteen thousand years ago.

Since 1910, however, it has been abundantly demonstrated that these older points of view are strongly at variance with the historical facts. For it is true that during the past four or five decades vast quantities of Stone Age remains, covering the entire span of prehistoric man's existence on earth—recently estimated at well over a million years—have been discovered in every part of Africa from Egypt, Libya, and the old Barbary States in the north to the Cape of Good Hope in the south, and from the Atlantic Ocean on the west, eastward to the Indian Ocean and the Red Sea. South Africa, the Rhodesias, Tanganyika, Kenya, Uganda, the Congo Republics, and the great basins of the Niger and the Nile—in short, the whole of the interior of Africa—are particularly well represented by such remains.

The same is true of even the Sahara and the Libyan deserts, which, thanks to evidence discovered during the past thirty or forty years, are now known to have been at long intervals very much better watered in Stone Age times than they are at the present day.

The prehistoric remains from these various regions include scores of fossil bones belonging to manlike apes or apelike men; hundreds of skeletons or skulls of true human beings that are so old that they have turned to stone; thousands of habitation sites and workshops where Stone Age Africans lived, loved, labored, and died; tens of thousands of paintings, engravings, and statuettes of animals and men, which were depicted on rocks or fashioned out of stone, ivory, mud, or bone by gifted artists who were among the earliest in the world; and finally, millions of hand axes, spearpoints and arrowheads, engraving tools, harpoons, and knife blades of various types. Among these tools and weapons are many which have been declared to be the finest objects of the kind ever made by prehistoric man.

Many specialists who have studied these artifacts and objects of art have been profoundly impressed, first, by the human skill which is reflected in many of them; second, by their remarkable resemblance to the same type of objects which have been discovered in Europe and Asia; and third, by the great age which can be surely assigned to the oldest of them. After taking all of the relevant facts into account, many of the experts on prehistoric man's handiwork have concluded that the relics of the Stone Age cultures of Africa are, as a whole, apparently as old and certainly as fine as any that have yet been discovered anywhere else in the world. Many of the more recent authorities who have given special attention to the matter are also of the opinion that most, if not all, of Africa's great prehistoric cultures originated in that continent and were not, as early scholars studying prehistoric culture formerly thought, importations from Europe or Asia.

As a matter of fact, after careful and extended studies of all of the relevant evidence, including minute comparisons of the cultures of the three continents, most of the ablest specialists in the history of Stone Age times think it highly probable that it was from Africa that many of the earliest prehistoric cultures of Europe and Asia were derived. In recent years, some of these specialists have gone so far as to suggest that the present evidence would seem to indicate that it was somewhere in the interior of the African continent that mankind first discovered and perfected the art of making tools and weapons out of stone.

In recent years much evidence has been assembled
which seems to indicate that the same may have been true
of painting and engraving on stone and of the arts of sculp-
ture and pottery-making as well. At any rate, most of the
earliest known objects representing these arts have been
found in Africa, or, if discovered in other parts of the world,
have been associated generally with skeletal remains belonging to the peoples of the so-called Negro, or Negroid,
or traditionally Africanoid types.

As surprising and revealing as the discovery and study
of Stone Age Africa's cultural remains have been, it is,
nevertheless, the recently recovered fossil bones of the
manlike apes and the apelike men and the skeletons of the
human beings which were so old that they had turned to
stone that have been the objects of greatest interest and
greatest surprise. Up to 1910 only one important discovery
of this kind had been made in Africa, but since 1910 hundreds of human fossils dating from the Old Stone Age have
been brought to light. These fossils, like the handiwork of
Africa's prehistoric men, have been found in all parts of
the continent.

Among these are many that have made a profound
impression upon, and which have been of the very greatest
value to, the specialists who have set for themselves the
engaging task of tracing the origin and evolution of the
human race. Although most of these remains have been
known to science for only a relatively few years, careful
study of them by competent authorities has already done
much to undermine confidence in the once widely held
hypothesis that Asia was the original cradleland of man.

It was Charles Darwin's opinion that Africa, rather
than Asia, was in all probability the birthplace of the human
race, and in the light of the remarkable discoveries that
have been made in the so-called Dark Continent in recent

years, many of the most eminent students of human origins are now disposed to believe that the great Seer of Downs may have been right.

In addition to the vast aggregation of archaeological and paleontologic remains to which passing attention has been directed, brief mention should be made here of a related group of materials that are of considerable interest to students of the early history of the human race. The reference here is to a relatively large number of skeletal remains, exhibiting what are commonly called Negro or Negroid traits, which have been discovered at numerous prehistoric sites in widely scattered regions in Europe and Asia. Some of these date from Stone Age times, but others belong to the later period known as the Early Metal Age.

In Asia such remains have been found in Palestine, Anatolia, Siberia, Arabia, Mesopotamia, Persia, India, Old Indochina, and the Philippines. In Europe what are described as Negro or Negroid skeletal remains have been discovered principally on Paleolithic or Neolithic or Aeneolithic sites in the Iberian Peninsula, Italy, Monaco, France, Belgium, Switzerland, Illyria, the Balkan states, and—according to the interpretations of some authorities—in Czechoslovakia, Mecklenburg, Silesia, Denmark, and southern Sweden. Evidence of a different type—chiefly paintings, statuettes, and other objects of art—indicates the presence of what are classified as Negro or Negroid types in Crete, Yugoslavia, Bulgaria, the Aegean archipelago, and on mainland Greece in protohistoric and early historic times. In association with some of the skeletal remains, there have also been found the bones of animals and the shells of certain aquatic creatures which are believed to have been of ultimate African origin.

The circumstances responsible for the presence of these alleged Negro or Negroid or traditionally Africanoid types in Europe and Asia are not definitely known. In earlier years, when it was widely believed that Asia was the original cradleland of all human types, it was supposed that most of them had originated in that continent and migrated thence to Europe. In the light, however, of our present knowledge concerning climatic changes which occurred in the Sahara and Libyan deserts in earlier times, there is an increasing disposition to believe that Africa was the ancestral homeland of these Negro or Negroid types, and that they were forced to flee to Europe and Asia by the drying up of much of their ancestral continent.

In the opinion of a number of eminent students of man's prehistoric past, the Negro or Negroid types represented by the aforementioned remains played a profoundly significant part in the ethnic and cultural history of Europe and Asia in earlier human times. Some think that it was these old Negro or Negroid or traditionally Africanoid stocks who introduced the first of the higher Stone Age cultures—the Aurignacian culture of the early Upper Paleolithic—into these continents; and, in support of this view, they point to the marked similarities between many of the Aurignacian stone implements and objects of art found in Africa on the one hand and in Europe and Asia on the other. Certain world-renowned authorities on human origins have ventured to assert that there are, indeed, adequate grounds for believing that some of the older Negro or Negroid types of Europe and Asia were the ancestral stocks from which some of the subsequent non-Negroid populations of these two continents were, in part at least, derived.

A number of the ablest anthropologists of modern times have explained in their writings that such developments were brought about through morphological modifications induced, in part at least, by environmental influences operating in accordance with well-established principles of natural law. An eminent Harvard authority has suggested that it was in this manner that an ancient dark-skinned and more or less Negroid stock was ultimately transformed into some of the peoples comprising that great ethnic complex commonly known as the Nordic race.

To the extent that library and laboratory facilities will permit, it is intended that students in the college of African studies at Nsukka will have the opportunity of becoming thoroughly acquainted with the already available evidence relating to the people and cultures of Africa and their influence on other parts of the world in Stone Age times; but over and above that, it is hoped that both the students and the staff of the college will find it possible to carry on independent field investigations which will bring to light new and significant African evidence capable of adding materially to the ever-growing armamentarium of knowledge which is rapidly resolving the riddle of human origins.

Written records, monumental remains, and other relics of the past relating to the peoples and cultures of Africa in historical antiquity and in later times are, reasonably enough, more varied and abundant than are the vast numbers of remains upon which Africa's Stone Age story is based. These more recent historical materials—so far as traditional notions about the continent are concerned—are of hardly less revolutionary import. Although many of these materials and their import have been well known to Africans for hundreds and in some instances for thousands of years, most of them were—with a few exceptions—almost totally unknown to the learned and the laity alike in the Western world until about one or two hundred years ago. In fact, knowledge of these materials almost down to the present day has been limited, in the main, to a small number of specialists who have been particularly concerned with the study of Africa's past. Even now when occasional bits of knowledge about these recently discovered historical materials reach the public eye or ears, there is often a disposition to receive them with skepticism, and at best with surprise.

For it is true that during the past century and a half, travelers, explorers, and archaeologists from Western lands have discovered in the expansive valleys of the Niger, the Zambesi, the Benue, the Limpopo, and the Upper Nile and its environs, as well as in the vast Sahara and the great basin of Lake Chad, extensive remains of hundreds of wholly ruined and completely abandoned or partly ruined and largely deserted cities and towns, which bear witness to the former existence of civilizations of types which are nowadays seldom associated in the popular mind of the Western world with the Dark Continent.

Some of these old cities and towns are known to have been established hundreds of years ago, and others, thousands of years ago. On or near these ancient or medieval habitation sites there have been discovered monumental remains of temples, tombs, palaces, public buildings, and other memorials of the past which indicate that they were erected by artisans and craftsmen who were highly skilled in the builder's art. Amid the disordered ruins and decaying remains of these old cities and towns have been found hundreds of old historical records written on processed skins or on slabs of stone, which tell us much about the peoples and nations by whom these dead and dying civilizations were built.

The more notable of the languages and scripts in which these old African historical records were produced were Cushitic hieroglyphics, Meroitic hieroglyphics, Meroitic cursive, Geez, or ancient Ethiopic, Amharic, Nubian Coptic, pure Nubian, and the enigmatic Tifanagh of the old Sahara. The contents of these native records are abundantly supplemented by invaluable historical information which has been preserved in the surviving annals of many contemporary peoples and nations who maintained more or less direct contacts with these now largely forgotten African civilizations when they were in the heyday of their development. These foreign records were produced by men of many climes and times, and were originally written in various scripts and tongues, including Egyptian hiero-glyphics, Egyptian demotic, Assyrian cuneiform, Hebrew, Sabaean, Sanskrit, Greek, Latin, Syriac, and Arabic as well as early forms of Portuguese, French, English, and Dutch.

Thanks to the information contained in these various and widely scattered but exceedingly valuable records of indigenous and exotic origin, as well as in hundreds of reports by African and foreign archaeologists and other specialists in antiquarian research, it is now possible to reconstruct in surprising detail the culture, and, to a large extent, the political history of literally scores of kingdoms and empires of various types, sizes, and claims to renown, which flourished in the "Heart of Black Africa" in historical antiquity, in the Middle Ages, and in early modern times.

The Kerma civilization of ancient Nubia, and the kingdoms of Napata, Meroë, and Axum, which were situated in the basin of the Upper Nile, were—according to the now available evidence—the oldest and most widely re-nowned of these nowadays little remembered ancient African states. The Christian kingdoms of Dongola and Alwah in Nubia and the Ethiopian empire of Prester John flourished in the same regions in the Middle Ages, and were hardly less renowned in their day than the ancient kingdoms which they replaced.

In Libya and regions farther to the west were the Garamantes and the wide-ranging Melano-Getulae and related peoples. In the same general region were the power-

ful Pharusii who went to war, say ancient authors, in
chariots "armed with scythes," and who, along with the
ancient Nigritae living in the basin of the Niger, took the
lead in destroying the ancient Tyrian (Phoenician) settlements of the West African coast.

In the Lake Chad basin was situated the great medieval empire of Kanem-Bornu, and farther west were the
Hausa States. Beyond these lay the great empires of Ghana,
Mali, and Songhai, which for centuries during the Middle
Ages were renowned far and wide as states of vast wealth
and unsurpassed power. Along the old Guinea coast and
stretching some distance inland were the remarkable Ibo
peoples and the astonishingly well-ordered kingdoms of
Benin and Yorubaland; and to the northwest flourished the
equally well-organized Mossi kingdoms and cognate states.

In the basin of the mighty Congo and its environs, the
earliest Europeans to visit these regions found, to their
surprise, a whole series of virile and dynamic kingdoms and
empires when they first arrived in these parts of the continent toward the end of the Middle Ages. Equally unexpected discoveries greeted the early "Admirals of the Ocean
Sea" during their initial voyages along the East African
coast. In the city-states of the Land of Zanj they witnessed
a flourishing civilization which, though different in its
cultural patterns, was quite as well developed in its basic
essentials—if not more so—as was their own. They also
heard echoes of the mighty inland empire of the Monomo-
tapa which they tried to invade and conquer but without
success.

In the national annals and surviving oral traditions,
occasionally supplemented by relevant information in
foreign records, are preserved the names of, and storied
details about, hundreds of kings and queens who guided
the destinies of their respective states over periods lasting

from a few decades to well over a thousand years. Among
the many kings and queens mentioned in these lists of
royalty there were, as there have always been in the history of every land, some rulers who were weak or bad or
both, whose whole lives were a shame to themselves and a
curse to their native lands. On these same lists of royalty
and in associated records are preserved, however, the names
and the storied details of the reigns of some of the ablest
statesmen and most benevolent potentates that are remembered in the recorded annals of man.

In the program of African studies at Nsukka the careers
of Africa's early rulers, both good and bad, as well as the
nobler, the normal, and the baser aspects of the civilizations
by which these rulers were produced, will be canvassed as
thoroughly as circumstances and the available sources of
information will permit. There is no need pretending that
this will always be done with absolute objectivity, for that
is an ideal that none who have labored in the quiet halls
of Clio—not even Thucydides—have been able to achieve;
but the guidelines will always be aimed, so far as is humanly
possible, in that direction.

The students at Nsukka will be ever urged to keep in
mind the fact that the African, like the rest of mankind,
has nothing to gain in the long run by suppressing the truth
and suggesting the false for chauvinistic reasons; more than
that, every effort will be made to demonstrate to the students that the known history of the continent makes it
quite unnecessary for even the most prideful to resort to
such practices. It will be emphasized that comparative
studies of the history of the peoples of the past make it
clear that the innate abilities, the cultural potentialities,
and the natural dispositions of all groups of men are now
and always have been—despite ethnocentric claims to the
contrary—basically the same in all of the major divisions
of humankind.

That is to say, at Nsukka it will be freely recognized that the "glory that was Greece," the "grandeur that was Rome," and the celebrated epics of many other non-African nations óf long ago are more than twice-told tales with a human appeal which, rightly enough, "time cannot wither nor custom stale"; but by the same token, it will also be recognized that the recent discoveries of the triumphs and failures of mankind form but a few fragmentary chapters in the total history of the human race. By taking all that is relevant into account, it will be seen that when the now available historical records, monumental remains, and other relics of the older cultures and civilizations of the early peoples of tropical Africa are objectively compared with the historical and prehistoric memorials of the other great divisions of the human family, it becomes clearly evident that genius and gentility, stupidity and savagery, are not now and never have been confined to any particular ethnic group in any restricted clime or continent, but are traits that have ever manifested themselves in all the peoples of the earth. In other words, knowledge of the real facts about Africa's past, when combined with the known history of other continents—as will be the practice at Nsukka—reveals that all races have, and have had throughout the ages, their sages and their simpletons, their saints and their sinners. In short, this approach to the study of the past demonstrates the universality of the wisdom and wantonness, the dignity and the depravity of man.

## SOCIAL VALUES

The academic context and content of the African studies program at Nsukka have been hurriedly summarized in the preceding remarks; we shall conclude this discussion with a few reflections concerning the social values of such a program. Let us begin by pointing out that under the influence of ethnocentrism, which is, latently at least, a well-nigh universal human trait, most men are disposed to view themselves through spectacles of their own making, and to judge their culture by norms and standards which they and their forebears have themselves selected or devised. There is, moreover, a disposition to regard other peoples and cultures with favor or disfavor in accordance with the degree to which they conform to, or depart from, the physical and cultural traits characteristic of themselves. In recent centuries, however, the vicissitudes of history have upset the order of nature by reversing or repressing natural and normal ethnocentric tendencies in many African peoples and peoples of African descent, both at home and abroad.

This unusual situation has grown out of the fact that during the last two or three hundred years many, if not most, African peoples—largely because of circumstances over which they had little if any control—have been forced to view in a very large measure their ancestral continent and themselves through the jaundiced eyes of myopic outsiders who were usually incapable of seeing things African in their proper light. To most of these ethnocentric intruders—the majority bent on plunder or adventure—Africa appeared to be hardly more than "a gigantic jungle filled with savage beasts and still more savage men"; but on which Nature, for some unfathomable reason, had bestowed many of her most priceless gifts with a lavish hand. In due course these adventure-bound fortune hunters from afar made themselves—thanks to their firearms—the masters of most of Africa under the ethnocentric guise of bringing the "blessings of civilization" to the "benighted" inhabitants of that "backward" but gold- and diamond-laden continent.

Controlling, as they did, the printing press and most

of the other mass media by which public opinion is formed, Africa's unwelcomed masters were able to convince the world at large that the African was indeed one of the most primitive examples of the "lesser breeds" of men; and was then, and always had been, incapable of lifting himself, under his own direction, above his "immemorial savage state."

In the effort to implant such an image of the African in the public mind, innumerable facts about Africa's present and past which were at odds with that objective were either ignored, or distorted, or suppressed. As a consequence, mankind in general, including many Africans, under the manifold influences of Western acculturation, accepted the exotic evaluations of the so-called Dark Continent and its peoples as gospel truth.

Contrary to what had been the situation in historical antiquity and in the Middle Ages—when Old Ethiopia and the *Balad es Sudan-sensu lato* were widely regarded as the cradlelands of civilization and the richest countries in the world—these same regions and their environs were transformed, as has been previously remarked, by Western machinations into "lands without a past," and almost universally believed to be, in terms of natural human needs, the poorest and least favored of all the great land masses of the earth.

Although many men everywhere were beguiled into accepting, to their spiritual detriment, these erroneous points of view, it was among unwary Africans that the greatest harm was done. Under the influence of these thoroughly fallacious but assiduously disseminated concepts and points of view, the prevailing attitude toward Africa and the African by non-African peoples was one of aversion, if not contempt. An even greater tragedy was the fact that under the spell of these altogether debasing concepts, many an African, both at home and abroad, was led not only to disdain the ways of his ancestral continent, but actually to demean and often, even, to despise himself.

He would often forsake his own norms, standards, and patterns of culture, which had served him and his kind quite effectively for countless generations, for exotic cultural yardsticks and borrowed social and personal practices which were seldom better and often much worse than those which had come down to him out of the past. Under the direct influence of Arnold J. Toynbee's teachings, he neglected the study of his own history on the assumption that it was unworthy of serious academic concern. The African was often an avid student of the "glory that was Greece" and "the grandeur that was Rome."

This attitude was most unfortunate, for as Cicero once remarked, in effect—with much truth—a man without a knowledge of his own history will remain forever a child; and with a larger context in mind the late Charles Seifert once trenchantly observed that "a race without a knowledge of its history is like a tree without roots." Each of these observations is but another way of saying that without a knowledge of their personal background or the background of the ethnic group to which they belong, few men are capable, particularly in hostile social environments, of maintaining their self-esteem or self-respect. Modern psychology has demonstrated that others seldom respect those who do not respect themselves.

In view of the ever-mounting volumes of anti-African propaganda to which the indigenous peoples of the continent were so long subjected and against which they were for decades in no position to present an effective defense, it is not surprising that so many Africans, with little or no knowledge of their past, permitted themselves to be misled into believing that they and their kind belonged to a lesser breed of men. However the situation may have been brought about, it was a social tragedy of the first magnitude nonetheless.

To be sure, there always have been strong and independent-minded Africans and Americans of African descent who not only successfully resisted all attempts to undermine their ethnocentric self-esteem, but who spent much, if not most, of their lives in efforts to keep the flickering torch of self-respect from being altogether extinguished in their less stalwart fellow men. The list is too long to be enumerated here, but among the pioneers of such endeavors in recent times, special mention must be made of the efforts of Edward Wilmot Blyden, Casley Hayford, John Sarbah, Apollo Kagwa, Samuel Johnson (of Oyo), Herbert Macaulay, and Solomon Plaatji.

Among those still living, or only recently deceased, W. E. B. Du Bois, J. A. Rogers, Dim Dolobson, Carter G. Woodson, J. B. Danquah, Jacob Eghareva, Nnamdi Azikiwe, Kwame Nkrumah, Jomo Kenyatta, and Mbonu Ojike deserve to rank high on the list. Nor must we neglect to mention here the large number of explorers, anthropologists, archaeologists, colonial officials, and the like of non-African descent whose labors in, or studies of, Africa—motivated in the main by intellectual curiosity rather than by the social and political implications of their efforts— have added immensely to the now available information about the African past.

But the world of today and tomorrow must not rest content with the heroic endeavors of those African pioneers who preserved against all odds their own abiding faith, and the less tenacious faith of their wavering contemporaries, in the enduring and meritorious realities of Africa's ancient ways of life; nor must the indigenous peoples of the great continent rely alone upon foreign investigators for the factual materials relating to their ancestral past. The African story will never be adequately known and adequately told until African devotees of Clio's art ferret out and interpret the facts for themselves.

It will be through taking the lead in sponsoring a program directed to that end that the college of African studies at Nsukka can best serve, in my opinion, not only Nigeria and the rest of Africa but the cause of truth in the world at large. Such a program by the college and by other African institutions of higher learning is, indeed, imperative if the African ethos handed down from the past is to be preserved, and if the indigenous peoples of the great continent are to attain the goals to which propitious destiny bids them to aspire.

# II. The Conversion Experience in Axum During the Fourth and Fifth Centuries

by Clifton F. Brown

Christianity has been the official religion of Ethiopia for over sixteen centuries. Throughout these centuries, the Ethiopian Orthodox church, next to the monarchy, has been the most important institution in Ethiopian history. It would be reasonable to assume that major periods in the history of such an important institution would have been the subject of constant investigation by scholars. Unfortunately, this has not been the case. Major periods and significant developments in the history of the Ethiopian Orthodox church have received only minimal attention by historians. Perhaps the most decisive period in the history of the church in Ethiopia, the introduction of Christianity into the Axumite Empire during the fourth and fifth centuries, has been almost entirely neglected by scholars.

For the historian and the theologian, knowledge of the instrumentality and the methodology by which a people receive a new faith claim is vital in understanding the new doctrinal and structural configurations the faith claim takes and the role the faith claim plays in the subsequent history of that people. In the case of those societies today that have retained their traditional lifestyles, the provenance and subsequent development of their religious constructs are all the more important in understanding the continual confrontation between tradition and innovation. Given the reality of growing opposition to the two pillars of authority and tradition in Ethiopia, the monarchy and the church, historical studies of aspects of both institutions would be beneficial in understanding the complexities of the situation in Ethiopia today.[1] It is the purpose of the present study to examine an important period in the history of the Ethiopian Orthodox church, the conversion experience of Ethiopia, or more properly, of Axum during the fourth and fifth centuries.

If the traditional date A.D. 330 is accepted for the official conversion of Axum, three events, all occurring in the previous eighteen years, would have substantially affected the Christian tradition that was accepted in Axum.[2] Prior to the year A.D. 312, Christianity, though spreading rapidly, particularly in the *Pars orientis,* was still suffering from a rather hostile attitude toward it on the part of the Roman authorities. And although under some Augusti, Christianity enjoyed some degrees of toleration, all too often the attitude of the state was one of hostility if not open persecution. In fact, the last, and by some accounts the greatest, persecution began as late as 303 under the emperor Diocletian. Yet ten years later, the co-Augusti, Constantine and Licinius, issued an edict of toleration making Christianity *religio licita.*[3] From this point onward, Constantine involved himself more and more in the affairs of Christianity. The culmination of this process can be seen in the dedication, in 330, of a second capital for the empire. The new capital, Constantinople, was designated by Constantine to be exclusively a Christian city.[4]

After the Edict of Milan, Constantine became more and more involved with protecting Christianity from both internal and external threats. At first, Constantine restricted himself to ensuring the Christians their civil rights and liberties. Shortly after the Edict of Milan, he wrote to Anulinus, proconsul of the Roman province in Africa, to restore to the Christians their property that had been previously confiscated.[5] Following this demand that the Christians be accorded all the rights of Roman citizenship, in a later letter to Anulinus, Constantine demanded special privileges for the Christians.[6]

From mere concern about the political welfare of the Christians, Constantine soon became involved in the internal quarrels of the church. Shocked by the Donatist schism,[7] Constantine wrote to Pope Miltiades (310-14) to make an inquiry into the whole matter.[8] Thus by the year A.D. 318 a precedent had been clearly established not only for imperial protection of Christianity but also for imperial intervention into matters that were purely doctrinal.

Around the year 318 a cleric of Alexandria came into conflict with his bishop, Alexander.[9] The cleric, Arius, had studied under Lucian of Antioch and had preserved the strong Antiochene bias which laid great stress on the unity of divinity and clearly distinguished the persons of the Trinity. Alexander and his successor, Athanasius, were staunch defenders of the Alexandrene tradition, and thus the Arian controversy, from the outset, bore the marks of the differences between the eclectic School of Antioch and the more exact and severe School of Alexandria.

At first, Arius' views were general and ambiguous. However, after his excommunication by a synod called by Alexander in 320 or 321, Arius began to work out a systematic Christology. In a letter to Eusebius of Nicomedia, Arius argued that Christ was a creature, that before He was created He was nothing, and that He was of a different substance than God the Father.[10]

Originally, Arianism was confined to the church of Alexandria and took the form of a discussion between the two opposed theological tendencies. Within a short time, both sides were engaged in writing letters to secure support for their views. Alexander sent letters to Pope Sylvester, the bishop of Antioch, the bishop of Berea, and many others.[11]

Arius, after fleeing Alexandria with the aid of Eusebius of Nicomedia, won the support of a council at Nicomedia and a council at Caesarea.[12] On Arius' return to Alexandria, the crisis was brought to a head. Constantine sent Hosius, bishop of Cordova, his adviser in ecclesiastical matters,[13] to investigate the dispute.[14] Hosius' peace mission was unsuccessful, and to further complicate the situation, fifty-six bishops from Palestine, Arabia, and Syria, assembling at Antioch to choose their new primate, took the opportunity, by a vote of fifty-three to three, to excommunicate Arius and the powerful bishop of Caesarea.[15]

In the early spring of 325, Constantine decided to summon a council representing all the bishops of the world to settle the dispute. The council opened at Nicaea on May 20, 325, at the imperial summer palace. At this first ecumenical council more than one hundred bishops came from Asia Minor, over thirty came from Syria-Phoenicia, less than twenty from Palestine, and three or four, in addition to two papal legates, from the West.[16] Little is known of the proceedings at the council. It is clear that Arius, his doctrines, and followers were condemned with little difficulty. While it was one thing to condemn Arius, it was quite another thing to frame an adequate definition of the orthodox position.

The difficulty arose from the fact that the Scriptures never fully explained the nature of the union of God the Father and God the Son. As Hughes observed, ". . . the

Scriptures had not been written for the purpose of confuting philosophically minded heretics."[17] During the course of the debates, some unknown bishop suggested the Greek word ὁμοούσιος (*homoousios*), that is, of the same substance or essence, to describe the relationship between the Father and Christ. There was some dissension over the use of ὁμοούσιος, since it did not appear in the Scriptures and it already had an unpopular history in the East.[18] But Constantine intervened in favor of the test word, and the creed was accepted by the council.

The intervention of Constantine was somewhat of a novelty.[19] Here we are presented with an instance where a catechumen ruled on the highest mysteries of the faith. Yet not a single bishop objected to the intervention of Constantine. By this action, the bishops acquiesced in the establishment of a new precedent—a secular authority ruling on purely doctrinal matters. Thus on the eve of the introduction of Christianity into Axum, three important developments had occurred. First, there was the adoption of Christianity as the cult of the Augusti. Next, there was the development of conflicting interpretations of the person and nature of Christ, and finally, the intervention of the secular authority into purely doctrinal matters.

The religious milieu in the Axumite Empire in the first quarter of the fourth century was complex. The Sabaeans, particularly the Habashat and the Aguezat, with their migrations from South Arabia to the Ethiopian highlands between 1000 and 400 B.C., had brought with them their religious customs. The chief deities of these Semitic peoples included Sin, or Almuqah (the moon god), Ashtar (the Venus star), and the Shams. Worship of Sin and Ashtar was centered in the Ethiopian highlands at the Sabaean city of Yeha. With the rise of Axum, a transformation of the names and functions of the old Sabaean gods took place. A trinity, comprised of Ashtar (Venus), Bahr, the sea god, and Medr, the earth god, was established. The patron of later kings of Axum in the pre-Christian era was Mahrem, god of war. The importance of the rise of Axum and the development of its indigenous civilization has been placed in perspective by Czeslaw Jesman's statement that "The Sabean influence was less pronounced than was supposed until recently by Western scholars, even though the same god, Ashtaroth Aouda, and Almuqah—the supreme moon divinity—was worshipped on both sides of the Red Sea."[20]

In the early pre-Axumitic or Sabaean period the position of high priest and governor was invested in an individual called the *mukarib*. Later, the importance of the position of the *mukarib* was diminished by the evolution of the position and title of *malkana* (king). This transformation evidently indicated the emergence of independent local personal control in the northern Ethiopian highlands.[21]

Among the indigenous Cushitic population, the Agaw, the worship of the serpent (*Arwe*), was widespread. Also among the Agaw were religious practices involving the worship of the sky god and numerous spirits inhabiting hills, trees, rivers, and fire. Sources from a later period have indicated that these cults were dominated by a large number of priests who possessed significant social and political powers. The source of their power over the local inhabitants emanated from their ability to communicate with the various deities and spirits.[22]

Another religious element in pre-Christian Axum was Judaism. In the *Kebra Nagast,* the national epic of Ethiopia, the introduction of Judaism into Axum was attributed to Makeda, Queen of Sheba, and her promise to King Solomon that "From this moment I will not worship the sun, but will worship the creator of the sun, the God of Israel."[23] In contemporary Ethiopia, the Queen of Sheba narrative has been regarded by many as the authentic version of the means by which Judaism was introduced into Ethiopia. In a recent Ethiopian publication is found the following noncritical evaluation of the narrative: "Information about the introduction of Judaism into Ethiopia is found in the *Kebra Negest*, (*The Glory of the Kings*). The visit of the Queen of Sheba to King Solomon in Jerusalem is recounted there."[24] In Article 2 of the Revised Constitution of Ethiopia, constitutional sanction has been given the narrative by restricting the imperial dignity to "The line of Haile Selassie I, descendant of King Sahle Selassie, whose link descends without interruption from the dynasty of Menelik I, son of the Queen of Ethiopia, the Queen of Sheba, and King Soloman of Jerusalem."[25]

Discounting the Queen of Sheba narrative, there were two possible routes by which Judaism may have been transplanted to Ethiopia by Jewish migrants. One possible route of infiltration was through Upper Egypt. This route, because of inadequate documentation, has generally been discounted.[26] The second route, via southern Arabia, was probably the chief avenue by which Jewish elements migrated to Ethiopia.[27] Although the subsequent impact of Judaism was significant in Axum, its initial converts were not the Axumites but the unsemitized Agaw population to the south of Axum.

A final religious manifestation in pre-Christian Axum was the introduction of the deities of the Greek pantheon. As early as the first century A.D., Hellenic culture had made significant headway in Axum. The unknown author of *The Periplus of the Erythraean Sea* wrote that King Zoscales (circa A.D. 50) was well acquainted with Greek literature.[28] The Hellenization of religion in Axum reached its peak during the late third and early fourth centuries. However, it appears that this process affected only the court circles in Axum and thus was probably a manifestation of an imperial cult. The fourth-century King Ezana referred to himself as "the son of the invincible god Ares" (υἱὸς θεοῦ ἀνικήτου Ἄρεως).[29] In a later inscription describing Ezana's campaign against the Tsarane was a description of the way Ezana gave an offering of thanksgiving for the successful culmination of his campaign to Mahrem, the Axumitic name for Ares.[30]

By claiming descent from Ares (or Mahrem), the rulers of Axum were ascribing to themselves a quasi-divine status. The implications of this were twofold. First, it gave a sacred aura to their person and divine sanction to their regime. More importantly, it meant that as the human representative or manifestation of divinity they took precedence not only over the nobility but also over the cultic priesthood. Thus on the eve of the conversion experience the precedent of a symbiotic relationship between religion and the political authority in Axum was well established.

The date for the earliest contact of Axum with Christianity has often been given as the first century A.D. This date has been suggested on the basis of the New Testament account of the conversion of a high official of Candace, queen of the Ethiopians (Acts 8:26-39). This reference to Candace as queen of Ethiopia was anachronistic and probably represented the result of a conflation of the Candace-Sheba and the Solomon-Alexander stories.[31] However, in Ethiopia the tradition developed that the official returned to Ethiopia and converted the people.[32]

A more accurate account of the initial conversion of

Axum was provided by the contemporary church historian Rufinus. His account was repeated in the church histories of Sozomen, Theodoret, and Socrates.[33] According to the account of Socrates, one Meropius of Tyre and two boys, Edesius and Frumentius, on landing on the Ethiopian coast, were captured by the local inhabitants. Meropius was killed but the two boys were taken to the court of the king.[34] Edesius became cupbearer to the king, and Frumentius was entrusted with the care of the royal records. When the king died, the widowed queen persuaded Edesius and Frumentius to act as advisers during the minority of her son. During the regency, Frumentius, a Christian, had churches built in the city. When the young king achieved his majority, Frumentius and Edesius turned the administration of the kingdom over to him. Edesius returned to his native Tyre, but Frumentius journeyed to Egypt to persuade the patriarch of Alexandria, Athanasius, to send a bishop to Ethiopia. Athanasius persuaded Frumentius to accept the episcopal dignity, and after his consecration, Frumentius returned to Ethiopia as its first *Abun,* or bishop.

The young king referred to in the accounts of Rufinus, Socrates, Sozomen, and Theodoret has been traditionally identified as Ezana (circa 325-50). Substance has been given to this tradition through examinations of the three inscriptions of Ezana's reign. In the first two inscriptions, Ezana claimed descent from Ares or Mahrem.[35] In the third inscription, there was a substantive change in language. Ezana no longer claimed descent from Ares. Rather, his position as king was secured "By the power of the Lord of Heaven, Who in heaven and upon earth is mightier than everything which exist."[36] In this inscription a change in the outlook of Ezana was clearly discernible. A new humility and a concern for justice and mercy can be seen in the concluding section of the inscription.

> May the Lord of Heaven make strong my Kingdom! And as He had this day conquered for me my enemy may He conquer for me wheresoever I go. And as He has this day conquered for me, and had overthrown for me my enemy, I will rule the people with righteousness and justice, and will not oppress them.[37]

Further confirmatory evidence of Frumentius' presence in Axum and of Ezana's conversion has been provided in a letter preserved by Athanasius. The letter was from the Augustus Constantius, the Arian son and successor of Constantine, and was addressed to Ezana and his brother Saizana.[38] In this letter, Constantius urged Ezana and his brother to send Frumentius back to Egypt for reexamination by the Arian patriarch George.

Particular attention must be paid to the fact that Abuna Frumentius, called in Ethiopia *Abba Salama, Kassaté Berhan* (Father of Peace and Revealer of Light), was consecrated by the patriarch of Alexandria, Athanasius. With Frumentius' successor, Minas, the appointment was again made by a patriarch of Alexandria, and in this instance the appointee was apparently an Egyptian.[39] Here was represented the beginning of Egyptian jurisdiction over the Ethiopian church. This factor was to have a profound effect on the development and character of the Ethiopian church.

The Alexandrene patriarchate, unlike the other Eastern patriarchates, was highly centralized. In Egypt only the patriarch had the right to consecrate bishops. The metropolitans had only delegated authority and could not act independently of the patriarch even in their own provinces.[40] The patriarchs of Alexandria, consequently, made every effort to see that the *Abun* in Ethiopia remained subordinate to them. To this end, the Egyptians forged a canon of the Council of Nicaea. The forty-second pseudo-canon of the Council of Nicaea prohibited Ethiopians from holding hierarchical positions.[41] In the *Fetha Nagast* (*The Legislation of the Kings*), the medieval constitution of Ethiopia, the Egyptians re-introduced this manifestation of religious imperialism.

> As for the Ethiopians, a patriarch shall not be appointed from among their learned men, nor can they appoint one by their own will. Their metropolitan is subject to the holder of the see of Alexandria, who is entitled to appoint over them a chief who hails from his region and is under his jurisdiction.[42]

The conversion experience in Axum differed greatly from the conversion experience of the Roman Empire. In the Roman Empire the initial converts were from the lower socioeconomic levels. However, in Axum the conversion experience began with the king and the royal family and filtered down to other segments of the population. Thus from the very beginning the king became chief advocate and defender of the church. Unlike Christianity in the Roman Empire, Christianity in Axum never experienced persecution by the state. The king from the first had been *defensor orthodoxae*.

In Axum, from the pre-Christian period onward, it was evident that religious and political or civil institutions developed a symbiotic relationship. This tradition was preserved after the conversion of Ezana. Ephraim Isaac has perceptively observed "Especially in its administration, the Ethiopian church has been geared from the beginning to maintain a religious attitude that permits both deep spiritual fervor and a sense of duty and obligation to the state."[43] In return, the king was to act as protector of the church.[44] The pagan designation of "son of the invincible god Ares" was substituted with the designation "elect of God."[45] This new designation represented not only an honorary title but suggested that the king had certain jurisdiction over the church. Constantius' letter to Ezana and his brother, asking them to send Abuna Frumentius to Egypt, has suggested the extent to which the king had jurisdiction over church affairs.[46] The role of the king in church affairs was also, no doubt, increased by the fact that the highest ecclesiastic, the *Abun*, was an alien.

The conversion of Ezana provided Axum with a unique identity and a holy cause. No longer was expansion of the kingdom merely a means of increasing the prestige of a king or the wealth of the state. Justification for expansion was now cloaked in the lofty idealism and religious fervor of spreading the true faith. A variant of this fervor can be seen during the reign of Kaleb (514-42).[47]

After the expulsion of the Axumites from South Arabia circa 375, the Himyarites, with their capital at Zafar, became quite powerful in the area. In the early sixth century one of the kings of Himyar, Dhu-Nuwas, converted to Judaism and began a systematic persecution of Christians. After the extermination of the Christian population in Nagran in 523, pressure was placed on Kaleb by both the Byzantine emperor, Justin I,[48] and the patriarch of Alexandria, Timothy,[49] to undertake the relief of the Himyarite Christians. These requests presented Kaleb the opportunity of not only aiding his beleaguered coreligionists but also the opportunity of reasserting Axumitic control over Yaman. Consequently, in 524, Kaleb and his army crossed the Red Sea.[50] Kaleb defeated Dhu-Nuwas and ended the persecution of Christians. Once the goal of his crusade had been accomplished, rather than withdraw his forces, Kaleb proceeded to subjugate the rest of Himyar and placed over the area as his viceroy a Christian Himyarite, Esimphaeus.[51] Although the period of Axumitic control of Himyar was short, the political ramifications of this manifestation of imperialism were enormous.[52] The Axumitic kings were henceforth regarded by the Byzantines as among the champions of the Christian world.[53]

Although Arianism had been condemned at the Council of Nicaea and Arius and two followers were exiled after the council, bishops began to question the orthodoxy of using ὁμοούσιος. In the autumn of 325, Eusebius of Nicomedia and Theognis of Nicaea withdrew their signatures from the condemnation of Arius, and by 328, Eusebius of Nicomedia had assumed leadership of the anti-Nicene party. Athanasius, who had become patriarch of Alexandria June 8, 328, and who would later consecrate Frumentius as *Abun*, became leader of the Nicene party. Though Athanasius had the support of the West, in the East the Arians, under Eusebius of Nicomedia, gained in strength. Over a dozen episcopal sees, from Palestine to Thrace, saw their pro-Nicene bishops deposed and replaced by Arians in a series of synods held between 326 and 335.[54]

Constantine himself wanted Arius readmitted to the church in hopes that such an action would end any further contention. At first approaching Athanasius through Eusebius of Nicomedia, upon rebuffs, Constantine angrily wrote to Athanasius that if he refused to readmit Arius to communion, he would "forthwith send someone who at my command shall depose you and drive you into exile."[55]

In 332, Athanasius was called to Nicomedia to answer charges laid against him in 331 by four Meletian bishops. Tried for bribery and sacrilege, Athanasius was acquitted.

These efforts by the Meletians to be rid of Athanasius led to the union of the Meletians with Eusebius of Nicomedia and others working for the readmission of Arius to the church.[56] The union of these forces, in addition to the attitude of Constantine, resulted in the first deposition of Athanasius at the Council of Tyre (335) and the first of Athanasius' exiles.[57]

When Constantius became sole Augustus in 350, his pro-Arian sympathies became the foundation for a new attack on the pro-Nicene position. Almost immediately, attacks were renewed against Athanasius.[58] At a series of synods, Arles in 353, Milan in 355, and Béziers in 356, Athanasius was again deposed.

It was shortly after the Synod of Béziers that Constantius wrote to Ezana and his brother requesting them to send Frumentius to Egypt. There were two reasons behind this request. Abuna Frumentius, since he had been consecrated by Athanasius, was a metropolitan of the church of Alexandria. Since Athanasius had been deposed, Constantius wanted Frumentius to acknowledge his Arian choice, the patriarch George, as the legitimate patriarch of Alexandria.

On this point Constantius wrote:

> Send therefore speedily into Egypt the Bishop Frumentius to the most venerable Bishop George, and the rest who are there, who have especial authority to appoint to these offices, and to decide questions concerning them. For of course you know and remember (unless you alone pretend to be ignorant of that which all men are well aware of) that this Frumentius was advanced to his present rank by Athanasius, a man who is guilty of ten thousand crimes. . . .[59]

Also, since Frumentius had been consecrated by Athanasius, Frumentius was, no doubt, a pro-Nicene. Thus Constantius was interested either in changing the theological position of Frumentius or, failing to do that, in replacing him with an anti-Nicene *Abun*. On that point Constantius wrote:

> But I am sure that Frumentius will return home, perfectly acquainted with all matters that concern the Church, having derived much instruction, which will be of great and general utility, from the conversation of the most venerable George, and such other of the Bishops, as are excellently qualified to communicate such knowledge.[60]

No indication of whether Ezana answered the letter or not, has survived. However, Frumentius did not go to Egypt, and in this fact Ezana not only acted as the protector of the *Abun* but, by not forcing Frumentius to go to Egypt, ruled on the orthodoxy of Frumentius.

The Arian controversy ended when the Ecumenical Council of Constantinople in 381 agreed to accept the Nicene formula.[61] The theological peace that followed the Ecumenical Council of Constantinople was threatened by the two opposing views of Nestorius, patriarch of Constantinople, and Cyril, patriarch of Alexandria.[62] Nestorius, as was one of his predecessors, Saint John Chrysostom, had been a student at Antioch and had subscribed to the Antiochene view that emphasized Christ's humanity as well as Christ's divinity.[63] Cyril, in 429, attacked Nestorius and his teachings in an Easter letter to his bishops and in an encyclical to the Egyptian monks. This action by Cyril was followed by an appeal by both Cyril and Nestorius to Pope Celestine (422-32) in Rome. When a Roman synod, under the authority of Celestine, condemned the views of Nestorius (430), Cyril, acting as the agent of Pope Celestine, gave Nestorius ten days after receiving the notice of his condemnation to recant.[64] Nestorius, in an effort to publicize his ideas and in an effort to silence Cyril's claim that his views were heretical, persuaded Emperor Theodosius II to call a third general council of the church. This council, the Ecumenical Council of Ephesus in 431, condemned the views of Nestorius and deposed him.

Though Nestorianism had been officially condemned, the danger that Nestorianism represented was ever present. Cyril, to combat that danger, continued to emphasize the Alexandrene position of the human made divine in Christ. His watchword was that there was one *physis*, or nature, in Christ.[65] To many followers of the Alexandrene school the belief of two natures could mean only one thing—a return to Nestorianism. The philosophical orientation which led these Alexandrenes, or, as they were called, Monophysites, to the conclusion that Christ had lost His human nature also led them to postulate that this human nature had been absorbed by His divine nature.[66]

The Monophysite controversy was brought to a head when Eutyches, an archimandrite of Constantinople, attacked Bishop Eusebius of Dorylaeum in Phrygia, an Antiochene in theological orientation. Eutyches revived the Alexandrene *Logos-Sarx* doctrine, that is, God incarnate as the human body (*sarx*) and the divine Logos, and by so interpreting Cyril's teachings, arrived at the conclusion that in the Incarnation the divinity and humanity of Christ were fused into one *physis*, one divine nature.[67]

Cyril had died in 444 and was succeeded by Dioscurus as patriarch of Alexandria. Dioscurus felt that the representatives of the Antiochene school were all Nestorians and allied himself with Eutyches. Opposed to the designs of Dioscurus was Flavian, who had become patriarch of Constantinople in 446. In a synod held in Constantinople in 448, under the presidency of Patriarch Flavian, Eutyches was deposed and excommunicated. In what seemed to have become a standard procedure in such cases, both Eutyches and Flavian appealed to Rome.

Pope Leo I (440-61), after reading the reports, found in favor of Flavian. Leo then wrote to Flavian his famous letter of June 13, 449, usually called the *Tome* or the *Epistola dogmatica,* indicating that he upheld Flavian's position. In this letter Leo held forth the common view of the West that in Christ there were two complete and full natures.[68] Dioscurus refused to accept the position of Leo, and to resolve the dispute another ecumenical council, the Council of Chalcedon, was called in 451.

Unlike the Council of Nicaea, the Council of Chalcedon proceeded rapidly with its work. First, the bishops deposed Dioscurus, and next they drew up a lengthy document reciting the Nicaeno-Constantinopolitan Creed, the letters of Cyril to Nestorius, and finally the *Tome* of Leo I. What followed has frequently been called the Creed of Chalcedon. In part this document reads:

> . . . one and the same Christ, Son, Lord, Only-begotten, to be acknowledged in two natures, inconfusedly, unchangeably, indivisibly, inseparably; the distinction of natures being by no means taken away by the union, but rather the property of each nature being preserved, and concurring in one Person and one Subsistence, not parted or divided into two persons, but one and the same Son. . . .[69]

Such was the symbol that has since been regarded by Greek, Latin, and most Protestant churches as the definitive or orthodox solution to the trinitarian and christological controversies. Yet for the Alexandrene school the settlement reached at Chalcedon represented heresy since it implied a duality of will in Christ. To the Alexandrenes the offensive clause, ". . . in two natures, inconfusedly, unchangeably, indivisibly, inseparably," became a war cry.[70]

After Chalcedon, popular violence became common in Egypt, and in both Egypt and Palestine large segments of the population were in practical revolution against both the ecclesiastical and the imperial authority of the empire. Proterius, the orthodox successor of Dioscurus in Alexandria, was murdered in an uprising of the people, and a Monophysite, Timothy Aelurus, was made patriarch. From the consecration of Timothy, the patriarchate of Alexandria became the center of Monophysitism and has remained Monophysite until today.

The initial stage of the conversion experience in Axum took place during the height of the Arian controversy. Though always on the periphery of this and other disputes, the Ethiopian church was affected by the development of each new stage of the controversies. The Ethiopian church's tie with Alexandria, though tenuous at times during this period, was, nevertheless, a reality. Thus if Alexandria under Athanasius was pro-Nicene, then the church at Axum was pro-Nicene. If under Dioscurus and his successors Alexandria was anti-Chalcedonian, then the church at Axum was anti-Chalcedonian. The Ethiopian church, in its fervor, even went to the extent of not only canonizing Dioscurus as it had Athanasius, but the church also named one of its anaphoras in his honor.[71]

During the period of the trinitarian and christological controversies, the infant church at Axum, in terms of internal development, was left to its own devices. The patriarchate of Alexandria was torn by dissension and was not able to offer much aid to support missionary activities in Axum. Consequently, during the period of the controversies, proselytizing activities in Axum were at a minimum.[72]

If A.D. 330 represented the date of the official conversion of Axum, the church remained in an embryonic state, and the effective conversion of the kingdom had to await the arrival of the Nine Saints, circa 480. The Nine Saints had been Monophysite confessors in Syria and after the Council of Chalcedon had been expelled from Syria.[73] After seeking refuge in both Egypt and Arabia, they finally settled in the Axumitic Empire. It was with the arrival of these monks that the substantive phase of the conversion of Axum began. During their sojourn in Egypt the monks had stayed at the monastery founded by Saint Pachomius. When the party of monks arrived in Ethiopia, they proceeded to introduce the practice of monasticism based on the Egyptian model. This development represented a turning point for the young Ethiopian church. Up to this point in time the church had not possessed an adequate organ for carrying out missionary activities. Monasticism met that need, and the monasteries in rural areas became the chief means by which the church combated paganism and acquired converts.[74] Abba Pentalewon transformed a pagan temple just outside the city of Axum into a church, Abba Afse transformed the famous pagan temple at Yeha into a church, and Abba Aragawi founded what is today the oldest monastery in Ethiopia, Debra Damo. Throughout the medieval period in Ethiopia, monasteries and their monks remained the chief agents for missionary activities.[75]

The Nine Saints, using a Syrio-Greek text, translated the Bible into the local language, Geez. This represented a great contribution to the missionary effort, since now the Bible would be in the language of the people. The Nine Saints also translated a number of other religious works into Geez.

Dogmatic treatises of the fathers of the church were collected and translated by the Nine Saints and entitled

*Qerlos,* or *Kerlos.* This collection of writings of the Fathers
was to become the foundation of the teachings of the
Ethiopian church. The *Qerlos* was Monophysite in its content,[76] and as the basis of church doctrine forever attached the Ethiopian church to the Monophysite cause.[77]
This factor, perhaps more than any other, reinforced Ethiopian dependence on Alexandria, since that patriarchate
was the chief proponent and defender of Monophysitism.
The true significance of the role of the Nine Saints in the
conversion experience of Axum was summarized by Budge
when he wrote that they "reformed the Faith."[78]

With the activities of the Nine Saints, the formative
period of the conversion experience of Axum drew to a
close. The relationship of the church to the political authority had been established during the reigns of Ezana
and his immediate successors. Through the literary efforts
of the Nine Saints, the Ethiopian church became firmly
established on the credal symbols of the councils of Nicaea,
Constantinople, and Ephesus as interpreted by Cyril and
Dioscurus. Ecclesiastical subordination to the church of
Alexandria, which originated in the consecration of both
Frumentius and Minas by the patriarchs of Alexandria,
was strengthened by the introduction of Egyptian monasticism and the reinforcement of Monophysitism by the Nine
Saints. Thus at the end of the fifth century, the essential
dogmatic tradition and institutional forms of historical
Ethiopian orthodoxy had been firmly established.

## NOTES

[1] See Revised Constitution of Ethiopia, arts. 126 and 127, *Negarit
Gazeta* (15th Yr.: 2, November 4, 1955), pp. 31-32.

[2] The Ethiopian historian Sergew Hable Selassie suggests A.D. 340
as the date for official conversion of Ethiopia. See Segrew Hable
Selassie, "Church and State in the Aksumite Period," *Proceedings*

*of the Third International Conference of Ethiopian Studies,* Vol. 1 (Addis Ababa: Institution of Ethiopian Studies, Haile Selassie I University, 1969), p. 5.

³ See "Exemplum constitutionis Imperatorum Constantini et Licinii," in Eusebius (Pamphili), *Hist. Ec.* x.5-4. This document is commonly called the Edict of Milan.

⁴ This event is significant since it meant that four of the five autocephalous sees, Alexandria, Jerusalem, Antioch, and Constantinople, were located in the East and that the new imperial city would become the chief rival of the premier see of the East, Alexandria.

⁵ "Ep. ad Anulinum," in Eusebius (Pamphili), *Hist. Ec.* x.5.

⁶ "Ep. ad Anulinum," in Eusebius (Pamphili), *Hist. Ec.* x.7.

⁷ The Donatist schism was created when a minority of bishops and clerics in North Africa denied the validity of the sacraments when they were performed by a *traditor.*

⁸ Eusebius (Pamphili), *Hist. Ec.* x.5.

⁹ The exact date is not known. See Jean Daniélou and Henri Marrou, *The First Six Hundred Years,* Vol. 1: *The Christian Centuries,* trans. Vincent Cronin (New York: McGraw-Hill Book Co., 1964), p. 248.

¹⁰ Arius, "Ep. ad Eusebium," quoted in Theodoret, *Hist. Ec.* i.5.

¹¹ See Alexander of Alexandria, "Ep. ad Alexandrum," in Theodoret, *Hist. Ec.* i.4; and "Epistula encyclica," in Socrates, *Hist. Ec.* i.6.

¹² Philip Hughes, *The Church in Crisis: A History of the General Councils, 325-1870* (New York: Doubleday and Co., 1964), p. 33.

¹³ Sozomen, *Hist. Ec.* i.16.

¹⁴ For the letter that Constantine sent with Hosius for Arius and Alexander urging them to end their dissension and bring peace to the East, see Eusebius (Pamphili), *De Vita Constantini* ii, 64-73. Part of the letter is also given in Socrates, *Hist. Ec.* i.7.

¹⁵ Hughes, p. 33.

¹⁶ Daniélou and Marrou, I, 251-52.

¹⁷ Hughes, p. 35.

¹⁸ Paul of Samosata, bishop of Antioch circa 260-72, had used the word when he represented the Logos as an impersonal attribute of God the Father. Paul of Samosata was a disciple of the Dy-

namic Monarchian School, a heretical group that, as a whole, held that Christ was the Son of God by adoption.

[19] It should be noted that the pagan emperor Aurelian was the first Augustus to issue an ecclesiastical ruling in his confirmation of Pope Victor's (189-198) condemnation of Paul of Samosata in 272.

[20] Czeslaw Jesman, *The Ethiopian Paradox* (London: Oxford University Press, 1963), p. 12.

[21] Jean Doresse, *Ethiopia* (London: Elek Books, 1959), p. 22.

[22] Taddesse Tamrat, "A Short Note on the Traditions of Pagan Resistance to the Ethiopian Church (14th and 15th Centuries)," *Journal of Ethiopian Studies* (10:1, January 1972), p. 138.

[23] E. A. Wallis Budge (ed. and trans.), *The Queen of Sheba and Her Only Son Menyelek*, translation from Bezold's edition of the Ethiopic text (London: Oxford University Press, 1932), p. 28. Cf. I Kings 10:1-13, II Chronicles 9:1-12, and Surrah xxviii. 15-45.

[24] *The Church of Ethiopia: A Panorama of History and Spiritual Life* (Addis Ababa: Published by the Ethiopian Orthodox Church, 1970), p. 2.

[25] Revised Constitution of Ethiopia, art. 2, *Negarit Gazeta* (15th yr.: 2, November 4, 1955), p. 3.

[26] See E. Ullendorff, "Hebraic-Jewish Elements in Abyssinian (Monophysite) Christianity," *Journal of Semitic Studies* (1:3, July 1956), pp. 210-20.

[27] Ibid., pp. 220-23.

[28] A. H. M. Jones and Elizabeth Monroe, *A History of Ethiopia* (Oxford: Clarendon Press, 1955), p. 22.

[29] From the inscription of Ezana concerning his deportation of six Bega rebels, quoted in E. A. Wallis Budge, *A History of Ethiopia, Nubia and Abyssinia*, Vol. 1 (Oosterhout N.B., The Netherlands: Anthropological Publication, 1966), p. 245.

[30] Inscription of Ezana describing his campaign against the Tsarane, quoted in ibid., p. 249.

[31] E. Ullendorff, *Ethiopia and the Bible* (London: Oxford University Press, 1968), p. 134.

[32] *The Church of Ethiopia*, p. 3.

[33] Sozomen, *Hist. Ec.* ii.24; Theodoret, *Hist. Ec.* i.21; and Socrates, *Hist. Ec.* i.19.

[34] In these accounts Axum (Ethiopia or Abyssinia) is referred to as India. This, no doubt, arose from the then current belief that Africa and Asia joined in the Indian Ocean.

[35] Quoted in Budge, *History of Ethiopia,* pp. 245-49.

[36] Ibid., p. 255.

[37] Ibid., p. 257.

[38] Athanasius, *Apol. ad Const.* 31.

[39] *The Church of Ethiopia,* p. 7.

[40] Jones and Monroe, pp. 35-36.

[41] *The Church of Ethiopia,* p. 9.

[42] *Fetha Nagast* iv.

[43] Ephraim Isaac, "Social Structure of the Ethiopian Church," *Ethiopian Observer* (14:4, 1971), p. 251.

[44] Ezana also made grants of land to the Church. See Richard Pankhurst, *State and Land in Ethiopian History* (Addis Ababa: The Institute of Ethiopian Studies and the Faculty of Law, Haile Selassie I University, 1966), pp. 22-23.

[45] Sergew Hable Selassie, p. 7.

[46] See Athanasius, *Apol. ad Const.* 31.

[47] Kaleb or Caleb (Ella Asbeha) has been canonized by both the Ethiopian Orthodox and the Roman Catholic churches.

[48] E. Ullendorff, *The Ethiopians* (London: Oxford University Press, 1960), p. 56.

[49] Budge, *History of Ethiopia,* p. 261.

[50] The year of the campaign is sometimes given as 525. See ibid., p. 262.

[51] Jones and Monroe, p. 30.

[52] Abreha, the second viceroy, revolted against Kaleb and established an independent regime in Himyar. In circa 540, Abreha engaged in an unsuccessful campaign against Mecca (Surrah cv. 1-5). Abreha did acknowledge Kaleb's son, Grebe Masqal, as his overlord. The Axumites were finally driven out of Arabia in circa 570 by the Persians.

[53] Doresse, p. 87.

[54] Daniélou and Marrou, I, 257.

[55] "Constantius ad Athanasium," quoted in Socrates, *Hist. Ec.* i. 27.

[56] See Sozomen, *Hist. Ec.* ii. 21.

[57] For a discussion of Constantine's role in these proceedings see Sozomen, *Hist. Ec.* ii. 28. Cf. Socrates, *Hist. Ec.* i. 34.

[58] In addition to his banishment at the Council of Tyre, Athanasius had been deposed at a synod at Antioch in 339 and again at the Council of Sardica in 343.

[59] Athanasius, *Apol. ad Const.* 31.

[60] Ibid.

[61] See "Symbolum Nicaeno-Constantinopolitanum," quoted in Philip Schaff (ed.), *The Creeds of the Greek and Latin Churches,* Vol. II: *The Creeds of Christendom with History and Critical Notes* (New York: Harper and Brothers, 1890), pp. 57-58.

[62] The exception to the generally peaceful state of the Christian world after Constantinople in 381 was the political dispute between the sees of Constantinople and Alexandria. This dispute led to the deposition of the patriarch of Constantinople, Saint John Chrysostom, in 403 and his death as an exile in 407. See Hughes, pp. 51-55.

[63] Karl Adam, *The Christ of Faith* (New York: New American Library, 1957), p. 52.

[64] Cyril, "Letter to Nestorius," quoted in Coleman J. Barry (ed.), *From Pentecost to the Protestant Revolt,* Vol. I: *Readings in Church History* (Westminster, Maryland; Newman Press, 1966), pp. 89-94.

[65] Hughes, p. 78.

[66] Ibid.

[67] Adam, p. 56.

[68] Leo I, "Tome to Flavian," quoted in Barry, p. 99.

[69] "Symbolum Chalcedonense," quoted in Schaff, p. 62.

[70] Ibid.

[71] Aymro Wondemagegnehu and Joachim Motovu (eds.), *The Ethiopian Orthodox Church* (Addis Ababa: Ethiopian Orthodox Mission, 1970), p. 55.

[72] Ullendorff, *The Ethiopians,* p. 101.

[73] The names of the Nine Saints are Abba Alef, Abba Sehma, Abba Aragawi, Abba Afse, Abba Garima, Abba Pentalewon, Abba Likanos, Abba Guba, and Abba Yem'ata. Of these the most famous are Abba Pentalewon, Abba Afse, Abba Aragawi, and Abba Garima.

[74] See *The Church of Ethiopia*, p. 7.

[75] For a description of the impact of monasticism on missionary activities during a later period, see Taddesse Tamrat, pp. 140 ff.

[76] Jones and Monroe, p. 38.

[77] E. Ullendorff, *The Ethiopians*, p. 102.

[78] Budge, *History of Ethiopia*, p. 259.

# III. George Washington Williams and Africa

by John Hope Franklin

Speaking before a Congress on Africa in Atlanta in 1895, the Honorable John C. Smyth, a former minister to Liberia, said that "Negroes are averse to the discussion of Africa, when their relationship with that ancient and mysterious land is made the subject of discourse or reflection." More than a generation later, in 1937, the distinguished historian Dr. Carter G. Woodson said that "Negroes themselves accept as a compliment the theory of a complete cultural break with Africa, for above all things they do not care to be known as resembling in any way those 'terrible Africans.'" Even Dr. W. E. B. Du Bois, in his autobiography, *Dusk of Dawn,* wrote of Blacks "who had inherited the fierce repugnance toward anything African, which was the natural result of the older colonization scheme. . . . They felt themselves Americans, not Africans. They resented and feared any coupling with Africa."

These sentiments, uttered at various times during the last three-quarters of a century by careful and thoroughly responsible observers, are in marked contrast to some views that Negro Americans have expressed in recent years. At

This address was delivered on May 7, 1970 as an inaugural lecture establishing a prize fund in honor of Rayford Whittingham Logan, professor emeritus.

59

the independence ceremonies in Nigeria in 1960, there were numerous Negro Americans in attendance; and they expressed almost boundless enthusiasm and delight with everything they saw. They made it quite clear that they wished to be identified with that race of people who, in achieving independence, were moving to an important position on the world stage. Several years later Negro Americans were expressing similar sentiments at the independence ceremonies of Zanzibar and of Kenya. If one such visitor found himself somewhat at a loss for words to respond to a warm greeting of one Nigerian who said, "Welcome home, brother," he appeared to have a warm feeling inside upon realizing that he could identify with his proud Black brother in the once legendary Dark Continent.

Does the rather overt if brusque manifestation of interest in Africa on the part of Negro Americans in recent years represent a significant modification of the sentiment described by Smyth, Woodson, and Du Bois in earlier years? Are the current pilgrimages to Africa on the part of Negro Americans—affluent members of the middle class as well as students working in the Peace Corps and Operation Crossroads—the result of a rather crude acceptance of Africans, now that they are heads of states, diplomats, delegates to the United Nations, and possible dispensers of favors and benedictions on their still rather hapless darker brothers of the New World? In one sense, the answer is yes; for the modern African states have captured the imagination of Black Americans and even thrilled them in simply realizing that Black peoples have risen to vaunted and enviable stations in life. Surely, in 1970 Negro Americans who could never have conceived that Black peoples would ever be rulers of nations and who could not previously identify with Africans as recently as a dozen years ago are delighted to be able to say today, "My friend, Chief so and

so, is the Minister of Finance of the African state of X"
or that "I have just returned from the African Republic of
Y, where I had luncheon with the Speaker of the House."

But in another sense, the answer is no. For there has
always been a deep interest, on the part of some Negro
Americans, in Africa, its past and present as well as its
future. Smyth, Woodson, and Du Bois were actually re-
proaching their fellows who seemed not to be as committed to a deep interest in Africa as they were. Even
before he was minister to Liberia, Smyth manifested a deep
interest in Africa. Dr. Woodson had long been a student
of African history and had written about it. One of his
most cherished ambitions was to compile an *Encyclopedia
Africana;* and at the time of his death in 1950 he was
working feverishly to realize this dream. Dr. Du Bois had
studied African history and culture even before he published his first book on the African slave trade in 1896; and
he was, in a very real way, the father of the Pan-African
Movement. Incidentally, it is relevant to this occasion to
observe that Dr. Rayford W. Logan, who was later to write
so extensively about Africa, was the principal assistant of
Dr. Du Bois in planning the early Pan-African congresses
immediately following World War I.

Just as the Negro liberation movement in recent years
has attracted vast numbers of people who, somehow, have
lost sight of the fact that the movement is more than a
century old and that it has been brought to its present
stage by the untold sacrifices and efforts of thousands of
pioneers, so does the current interest in Africa represent
the continuation of a tradition that was begun centuries
ago by highly imaginative, skillful, and resourceful Negro
Americans. This interest in Africa is not new. Rather, the
interest has become enlarged and now includes hundreds
of thousands who a few years ago could not have dreamed

that they could have any serious interest in the affairs of the so-called Dark Continent.

To recognize this recent upsurge of interest is not to reproach those who have discovered it. Negro Americans, with all their problems of survival, of gaining a measure of respectability, and of winning a semblance of their rights, had little energy and resources left to channel into the affairs of Africa. There was, moreover, the almost natural inclination—as Woodson and Du Bois implied—of avoiding identification with causes and peoples who apparently could do little if anything for them to relieve their plight. It would, nevertheless, be both unfair and inaccurate to suggest that the interest of Negro Americans in Africa is of recent origin or that it has been, from the beginning, banal and self-seeking.

There was scarcely a time when some Negroes in the New World did not entertain hopes that they would, some day, migrate to the land of their forebears. At times these hopes were inspired merely by the search for identity, for roots, for security. At other times they were viewed as the numerous manifestations of barbarity on the American scene. Paul Cuffe, the affluent Negro Quaker of Massachusetts, who early in the nineteenth century began to dream of ending his days as a migrant to Africa, held these dreams because of the nightmare of his experiences with the hypocritical claims of freedom and independence on the part of the American patriots during the American Revolution. John Russwurm, one of the first Negro college graduates and an early advocate of solving the problem of race in the United States, soon became convinced that Negroes had no future in the United States and became an ardent advocate of migration to Africa. "We consider it a waste of words to talk of ever enjoying citizenship in this country," he concluded. Thereupon, he emigrated to Liberia in 1829 to become the first superintendent of public schools in that country. In numerous other ways—as editor of the *Liberia Herald,* governor of the Maryland Colony, and a leader in the unification of Liberia—he sought to bring strength and stability to his adopted home.

Martin Delany, who had opposed colonization and had written against it, reached the conclusion in 1852 that migration to Africa was the only solution. "I am not in favor of caste," he said, "nor a separation of the brotherhood of mankind, and would as willingly live among white men as black, if I had an equal possession and enjoyment of privileges. . . . But I must admit, that I have no hopes in this country—no confidence in the American people, with a few excellent exceptions." He called on Negro Americans to join him in establishing a nation on the eastern coast of Africa. "The land is ours—there it lies with inexhaustible resources; let us go and possess it." The convention which Delany called to consider the problem met in Cleveland in 1854. Although the delegates were not specific in their desire to settle in Africa, they were enthusiastic about their African heritage, and they declared that they would not submit any longer to the domination of the white race, which, after all, "constituted but one third of the population of the globe."

It was, then, the bitter experience of Negro Americans in the United States that kept alive their interest in migrating to Africa; and that experience would continue through the nineteenth century and into the twentieth century. In 1883, when the United States Supreme Court declared the Civil Rights Act of 1875 unconstitutional, Henry McNeal Turner, former chaplain of the Union Army, former member of the Georgia legislature, and bishop of the A.M.E. church, made up his mind. "There is no manhood future in the United States for the Negro," he said.

"He may eke out an existence for generations to come, but he can never be a man, full, symmetrical, and undwarfed." Thousands of others reached the same conclusion. In 1877 several hundred Negro families in South Carolina joined up to go to Liberia. And later experiences moved others to resolve to go to Africa. After World War I, Marcus Garvey would point to the degradation of Black Americans and call on them to join him in the most ambitious back-to-Africa scheme the world had ever seen. Within a few years millions of Negroes were talking about Garvey's Universal Negro Improvement Association, and hundreds of thousands were taking his back-to-Africa proposals seriously. Their attachment to the Garvey movement and other Zionist movements reflected their despair and frustration more than it represented an active interest in migrating. In the final analysis, the interest of most of them did not seem to extend beyond the water's edge. But this was an interest that brought more Negro Americans into a closer consideration of things African than had ever before been the case.

For many years, however, there had been a small group of Negro Americans who did go beyond the water's edge, not necessarily for the purpose of migrating, but to do what they could to advance and improve conditions among their African brothers. These were the religious leaders who hoped to share with Africans their own view of the better life through religion. They had little or no assistance from their white coreligionists, who seemed unable to bring themselves to join in an interracial movement to bring the light of Christianity to the Africans. Nor did the white rulers of Africa relish the idea of Negro Americans undertaking to Christianize Africans, lest they upset the white man's ideas of "how a Black man was supposed to look, act, and sound." But David George went there in 1792 to organize the Baptist church in Sierra Leone. Daniel

Coker took Methodism there in 1821. Lott Carey, the pru-
dent Baptist minister who saved his money and purchased
his own freedom, became a leading exponent of Christian
missions in the following decades.

Even if Negro American missionaries did not enjoy a
great success in converting their Black African brothers,
their presence in Africa had a profound and lasting effect
on Negroes in the United States. It kept alive their interest
in Africa. As missionaries returned and told of their experiences, as they sought continued support for their overseas enterprises, as they underscored the continuing cultural, racial, and even political bonds between Negro
Americans and Africans, they convinced many Negro Americans that Africa was indeed worthy of their interest and
consideration.

Perhaps the best example of the early and continuing
interest, not altogether selfish, is manifested in the career
of George Washington Williams, the first major Negro
American historian. Williams, who was born in Pennsylvania in 1849, had little education during his early years.
His parents seemed constantly on the move from one Pennsylvania town to another and finally to Massachusetts,
where he studied for several years in the public school and
academy in New Bedford. When he was fifteen, in 1863,
he ran away from home, assumed the name of an uncle,
and enlisted in the United States Colored Troops. The
examining surgeon, aware of the fact that Williams' zeal
to fight far exceeded his age, rejected him; but after much
pleading on the part of Williams, the surgeon relented.
During the war Williams was severely wounded and received an honorable discharge from the service. As soon
as he recovered he reenlisted and saw action in several
battles during the closing months of the war.

Shortly after the war Williams was ordered to be mustered out, but adventure and wanderlust had completely captivated him, and he enlisted in the Mexican army where he advanced from orderly sergeant to assistant inspector general, with the rank of lieutenant colonel in the First Battery from the state of Tampico. In 1867, after the execution of Maximilian, Williams returned to the United States and entered the cavalry service of the regular army, serving in the Comanche campaign in 1867. The following year he left the army, and after a brief sojourn in St. Louis and Quincy, Illinois, he returned east, where he resumed his studies. First, he enrolled in Howard University, but within a year he was in the Newton Theological Seminary in Cambridge, where he graduated in 1874. At the commencement exercises he delivered the class oration, "Early Christianity in Africa," in which he demonstrated an intimate knowledge of the historical development of Africa in the early centuries of the Christian era. This interest in Africa would remain throughout his life.

In the years that followed, Williams' interest shifted from religion to business, law, and politics. For a while he was storekeeper in the internal revenue department in Cincinnati. He attended lectures at the Cincinnati Law School and studied in the office of Alphonso Taft, father of the future president. In 1881 he was admitted to the Ohio bar and was later admitted to practice before the Supreme Judicial Court in Boston. Meanwhile, he had entered Republican politics and in 1879 was elected to the Ohio legislature, where he served as chairman of the Committee on the Library and on several other legislative committees. These were his busiest years. He was minister, lawyer, contributor to a newspaper, legislator, and student of history. There, he began to write his two-volume *History of the Negro Race in America,* which was published in 1883. The appearance of this work was an event of unusual significance in publishing and literary circles. Because of the nature of the work, the critics were compelled to take it seriously; and if they did not always praise it, they were forced to concede that it was a unique and important work. Five years later he brought out his *History of the Negro Troops in the War of the Rebellion,* for which the *Literary World* offered the author "congratulations for the intelligence, discretion, and excellent workmanship with which he prepared the book."

The limited literary and financial success of his historical works by no means satisfied Williams, who was a man of burning ambition, of boundless energy, and with a determination to make his mark in the world. Even as he wrote his history he continued his interest in politics; and there can be no doubt that he was ambitious for some high office, elective or appointive. He was active in Republican politics during the 1880s and was well acquainted with President Chester Arthur and with Representative James G. Blaine. In the closing days of the Arthur administration, the president nominated Williams to be minister to Haiti. The Senate confirmed him on March 3, 1885; and Williams was sworn in the following day, a few hours before Grover Cleveland was inaugurated as president. This "midnight appointment" was widely regarded as a Republican trick designed to embarrass the incoming Democratic administration; and there is reason to believe that it did embarrass the Democrats. After some equivocation, they declined to permit him to execute the required bond and to take office.

This was, for Williams, a most bitter experience. At precisely the moment that he was about to realize one of his most cherished ambitions, he discovered that he had been the victim of whimsical, partisan politics. It was enough to discourage most men. But Williams was not easily discouraged; and surely, he would not permit one setback to dispirit him. He merely used this experience as the occasion to return to one of his earliest interests, Africa. Indeed, his interest in Africa had never flagged. He had studied African history while doing research on the history of the Negro people in America. In 1884, the year following the appearance of his history, he wrote a series of articles on African geography in which he disputed the Portuguese claim to the Congo. In the same year he appeared before the Senate Committee on Foreign Relations urging the passage of a resolution recognizing the International Association for the Congo as a friendly government. Within a few days the Senate passed such a resolution, and Williams assumed that his plea had the effect of influencing some of the senators. Greatly encouraged that United States recognition would have a salutary effect on the future of the Congo, Williams decided to take a more active part in the development of central Africa.

In the summer of 1884 he went to Europe armed with a warm letter of introduction from the secretary of state, Frederick T. Frelinghuysen. In August he made the first of several calls on Leopold, king of the Belgians. He consulted at length with the king about the labor system in the Congo and placed before him some suggestions for the use of Black Africans and even Black Americans in the development of the area. His suggestions seemed to meet with the king's approval. Doubtless, it would be good for the Belgians to have the support of a Negro American in their plans for the exploitation of the Congo, so long as he did not inspect too closely just what was going on in the Congo.

Williams was particularly concerned with the persistence of slavery and the slave trade in Africa. He hoped that if Belgium would take the lead in giving Africans in the Congo an opportunity to work as free men in the development of the region, it would be an admirable example for other powers to follow. He prepared an elaborate historical paper on the Congo in which he praised the establishment of the Free State in 1885 and urged the United States to join in assuming certain obligations regarding its sovereignty and neutrality. In 1889 he conferred both with President Harrison and John Sherman, chairman of the Senate Committee on Foreign Relations. Neither wanted to become involved in any scheme to guarantee the neutrality of the Congo Free State. They were, however, cordial to the idea of having an American delegate at the Antislavery Conference of the European Powers, called by King Leopold.

Williams wrote and spoke against slavery in Africa and urged Americans to follow the example set by the Quakers a century earlier. "They would not buy or use rice, sugar, coffee, cotton, or any other article they knew to be the product of slave labor. We can draw inspiration and instruction from the sublime action of the American colonies which passed the Non-Importation Act. We can refuse to send rum to the Arab with which to buy slaves and drug his hapless victims. We can talk against it, and pray God for light upon this dark subject which it is our duty to aid in settling."

In the autumn of 1889 Williams spent two months in Belgium attending the antislavery conference and conferring with the Belgians about labor problems in the Congo. In December he called at the White House and reported to President Harrison on the proceedings of the conference. He promised to prepare a memorandum containing reasons why the United States should ratify the General Act of the Conference of Berlin of 1885 recognizing the Congo Free State. Before he could complete the report, he had sailed again for Europe, en route to the Congo.

It is not clear precisely when Williams decided to visit the Congo. Surely, he had not indicated to the Belgians, during his recent visit, his intentions to go there. Perhaps he had been encouraged by certain Americans to make the visit. The president was cordial to him and apparently wanted as much information about the Congo as Williams could provide. S. S. McClure, the leading magazine editor of the time, was also interested; and he commissioned Williams to do a series of articles on Africa for his magazine. Williams also had a commission and, presumably, a healthy expense account from the railroad magnate Collis P. Huntington to survey the Congo and advise him on the feasibility of building a railroad across the Free State.

Williams proceeded to Brussels, where he made known his intention of visiting the Congo. Everything possible was done to dissuade him. "Officials who formerly greeted me cordially, now avoided me, and wrapped themselves in an impenetrable reserve," he reported. "An officer of the King's Household was dispatched to me for the purpose of persuading me not to visit the Congo. He dwelt upon the deadly character of the climate during the rainy seasons, the period and hardships of travelling by caravans, and the heavy expenses of the voyage. . . . I simply replied that I was going. After this the King sent for me, and received me cordially. I did not care to lead up to the conversation on the Congo, and consequently I strove to turn the conversation to other topics. But soon I saw that there was but one thing about which His Majesty cared to converse, and I made up my mind to allow him to do all the talking."

The king explained the difficulty of traveling and living in the region and urged him to postpone his trip for at least five years, and in return the king would see that

Williams would receive, in Brussels, all the information he desired about the Congo. The more the effort was made to dissuade him, the more determined Williams was to go; and the king told him that if he persisted he would not be allowed to go on a state steamer.

That presented no problem to Williams. He crossed the channel to England, purchased all necessary supplies in London, and sailed from Liverpool at the end of January 1890. The trip to Africa was the realization of a lifelong ambition for Williams, and he intended to make the most of it. The voyage from Liverpool to Boma, the capital of the State of Congo, occupied fifty-three days, during which time Williams was able to stop at most of the important ports on the west coast of Africa. He visited Sierra Leone; Sino, Baraby, and Cape Palmas in Liberia; the Ivory Coast, the Slave Coast, the Gold Coast, and Bonny, at the mouth of the Niger River in present Nigeria; Calabar, and the Cameroons, the Portuguese island of São Tomé, and Gabon in French Equatorial Africa. Williams was distressed to observe the selfish and oppressive rule of the Liberians. He was shocked to notice the hostility to the British on the part of the Portuguese, and he was thrilled to have an interview with an African king on the Slave Coast. He visited churches, trading posts, villages in the hinterland; and he talked with many European businessmen trading in Africa.

Finally he reached the Congo and spent four months traveling there. He went from the mouth of the Congo River at Banana to its headwaters at Stanley Falls; from Brazzaville on Stanley Pool to the Atlantic Ocean at Loango. In all he traveled some 3,266 miles in the Congo. It was a grueling experience, but the only complaint that Williams had was that he, together with his staff of eighty-five Congolese aides, sometimes suffered from fatigue, hunger, and heat. On one occasion it appeared that the courage of his men would "abate" and Williams considered executing two of them, but "with firmness and heroic suffering without a murmur I triumphed." "Sometimes," he said, "I was crossing plains which stretched days before me, as level as our own prairies; again I struggled for four days through the dense, dark and damp forest of Muyambu, where it rains every month in the year. Sometimes I came upon villages of friendly natives who offered me a house and food if I would honor them by remaining over night with them; and again hostile natives warned me to move on, denying me food and entertainment. But I never consented to go. I knew too well the virtue of my modern firearms; and I usually gave them to understand that I wanted food for my people and would pay for it, and if it were not forthcoming within one hour I would come and take it. Hungry men are usually heroes for the hour, and I always got food when there was any to be had."

It was also a disenchanting experience, resulting in a public denunciation by Williams of both King Leopold and His Majesty's principal emissary in the Congo, Henry M. Stanley. In July 1890, from Stanley Falls in the Congo, Williams wrote an "Open Letter to the King of the Belgians." At last he knew why Leopold did not want him to visit the Congo. In the first place, Leopold's title to the area was tainted by frauds of the grossest character. Williams stated: "Your Majesty's government is deficient in the moral, military and financial strength to govern a territory of 1,500,000 square miles," he continued; "guilty of violating its contracts made with its soldiers, mechanics, and workmen; the courts of your majesty's government are abortive, unjust, partial, and delinquent; your majesty's government is excessively cruel to its prisoners." The bill of particulars contained twelve charges of the most serious nature; and Williams concluded by telling the king, "All the crimes perpetrated in the Congo have been done in your name, and you must answer at the bar of public sentiment for the misgovernment of the peoples whose lives and fortunes were entrusted to you by the Conference of Berlin of 1884-1885."

Williams wrote a lengthy report to Collis P. Huntington and his colleagues, entitled "Report on the Congo Railway." In it he reviewed the procedure by which the Free State had, in 1887, chartered the Compagnie du Congo pour le Commerce et l'Industrie to survey and build a railroad. The terms were liberal, and the company received almost a half-million acres of choice land. The company had spent more time exploiting the resources of the land than in surveying and building the railroad. At the end of almost four years, "not one mile of road-bed has been laid, and only twenty miles of survey has been completed."

Williams declared that the proposed railroad was the result of the "wild, irresponsible advice" of Henry M. Stanley to King Leopold. It could not be built for the amount specified (sixteen million francs) or in the time specified (three years). It would require at least forty million francs and, under the most favorable conditions, at least eight years. Of Stanley, Williams said, "When he describes things and persons he displays the ability of an able correspondent. But the moment he attempts to deal with figures and trade, he becomes the veriest romancer. . . . Modern history records nothing equal to the speculation of Mr. Stanley. . . . And while I have an interest in the civilization of Africa equal to any person's, I cannot be silent, or suffer to pass unchallenged statements calculated to mislead and deceive the friends of humanity and civilization." He encouraged Huntington by saying, "The Congo railway ought to be built, and from the bottom of my heart I hope it will be." He clearly implied that what was needed was the genius and wealth of Collis P. Huntington and the well-remunerated advice of George Washington Williams!

The third report of Williams was written at Luanda, Angola, and was addressed to President Harrison. In it he reviewed his long interest in Africa and the President's interest in his investigations. He declared that Leopold's claim to the Congo was based on spurious treaties, supposedly made by Stanley with more than four hundred kings and chiefs. "And yet many of these people declare that they never made a treaty with Stanley, or any other white man; that their lands have been taken from them by force; and that they suffer the greatest wrongs at the hands of the Belgians." He said that he hoped that American interest in the welfare of the state and its people would continue and that this interest would be guided by noble and unselfish motives. The people of the United States, because of their earlier interest in the Congo have a "just right to know the truth . . . respecting the Independent State of Congo, an absolute monarchy, an oppressive and cruel government, an exclusive Belgian colony, now tottering to its fall. I indulge the hope that when a new government shall rise upon the ruins of the old, it will be a simple, not complicated; local not European; international, not national; just, not cruel; and casting its shield alike over black and white, trader and missionary, endure for centuries."

After Williams completed his mission in the Congo, he proceeded to Angola, Southwest Africa, where he spent several weeks resting and writing. During his sojourn in the city of Luanda he had an opportunity to observe at close hand Portuguese rule in Southwest Africa. The Black slave, he reported, had a miserable existence, but Williams was pleased to see that the considerable number that were becoming free immediately enjoyed what he described as complete equality. "There is more genuine, heartfelt democracy here," he wrote a friend, "than in your boasted America. Every Black man in Luanda has a vote at the municipal elections, there are mixed schools, there are no separate churches—a great thing for the Catholic religion —there are no separate grave yards." Williams was not deluded into thinking that European rule in Africa was a good thing, however. After making his observations regarding the progress of Black men in Angola, he said, "Notwithstanding all these things my cry is *Africa for the Africans!*" This conclusion was doubtless reached, in part, because of the convict system and the various labor schemes which he regarded as repressive in the extreme.

This trip, the last of his life, turned into a grand tour for Williams. Upon leaving Angola, he took a ship around the Cape of Good Hope to Algoa Bay, then up the east coast to Zanzibar, where he lived and worked for about six weeks. While there he was entertained by the British consul general, by the merchants and other leading citizens, and was made an honorary member of the English Club. He also had a private audience with the sultan. From Zanzibar, he proceeded northward, visiting Mombasa and Lamu in British East Africa, before going to Cairo, where he remained for several weeks in the spring of 1891. He concluded his trip by visiting Tripoli, Tunis, and Tangier.

In the late spring of 1891 Williams was back in London, doing research at the Public Record Office and preparing a lengthy manuscript on the Congo. When he left Africa his strength was greatly diminished by the strenuous activities in which he had been engaged; and old maladies, complicated by his wartime wounds, began to recur. En route to England he became friendly with a young English woman, traveling from India with her mother. By the time they reached England they had become engaged, although Williams had a wife back in Washington, D.C. When his health continued to deteriorate, the young lady and her mother accompanied Williams to Blackpool where, it was hoped, the sea air would give him strength. This move was too late; and on August 2, 1891, at forty-three years of age, Williams expired.

The death of Williams made little stir in the United States. The excitement in England was over the large inventory of African curios that he brought back with him and that were now to be sold at auction. "A unique and valuable collection," the advertisement read, "comprising copper knives, quaint daggers and swords, carved spears, ornamented paddles, shields, bows and arrows, ivory tusks and trumpets, brass rings for neck, ankles and wrists, fishing spears, and other interesting objects, obtained from the natives during an extended tour of exploration by Col. George Washington Williams, an American citizen, recently deceased at Blackpool." These items, a sort of "last hurrah" for Williams, told their own story of the great variety of African cultures that Williams had come to appreciate and to respect. Soon, however, the American public would learn of his defiance and bitter condemnation of the king of the Belgians for betraying Black Africans, of his advocacy of American support that might guide the Congolese to a new destiny of independence and self-respect, and of this final, heroic effort of George Washington Williams to learn more about the land of his fathers. He had not accomplished nearly as much as his boundless energy and indomitable will drove him to attempt; and in his enthusiasm he had cherished the futile hope that his own country could develop a "noble and unselfish" interest in Africa. But he had become one more witness to the continuing and increasing interest of Black Americans in Black Africans.

# IV.  We the Children of Africa in This Land: *Alexander Crummell*

by Otey M. Scruggs

The focus of this paper is Alexander Crummell, nineteenth-century Black clergyman and scholar, and his thought during the latter part of the century.† At that time Black people were faced with the perennial problem of an oppressive system of color caste and how they could overcome the systematic effort to dehumanize them. They asked themselves more insistently, Where do Black people fit into the world? What is to be our relationship with Africa? What is our relationship with white Americans? What are the means best suited for achieving the emancipation of Black people in a land bent on our degradation if not our destruction? What is to be the relationship of the educated few to the untrained many? These may not have been all of the concerns of all Black people, but in some way or other they occupied the attention of most. Crummell thought about all of these problems. Indeed, his special significance for that day may well be that having thought seriously about them since long before the Civil War, Crummell in a mature and systematic way articulated them to a growing middle-upper class of Black professionals and intellectuals. In an age of increasing fragmentation in

†I wish to thank my colleagues Professor Peter Marsh and, especially, Professor Michael Coray for help with ideas and in the organization of the paper.

American life, Crummell spoke to their deep need for community.

Alexander Crummell was born in New York City in 1819. He was born into that part of the free Black community that, organized around its churches, promoted "moral and intellectual improvement," established organizations to further this twin objective, and contributed to the antislavery cause. Through the community ran a powerful missionary impulse, the urge to regenerate the poor and the unchurched. Because these Black folk tended to view themselves as children of Africa in this land, they believed that Africa, too, had to be redeemed.

Young Crummell was powerfully affected by these currents. They received reinforcement from his education and preparation for his life's work: in the African Free Schools of New York City; at Oneida Institute, an interracial school of strong antislavery persuasion; in the Andover Theological Seminary, where he probably trained for his ordination into the Protestant Episcopal church priesthood in 1844. In 1853 Crummell graduated from Queen's College in Cambridge, England. The same year, he emigrated to the new black Republic of Liberia, where he remained for twenty years as a missionary of the Episcopal church and as a college and high school teacher. He worked with the American Colonization Society in the 1860s to promote emigration to Liberia. His principal concern, however, remained the evangelization of Africa, and after his return to the United States permanently in 1873 he continued to promote the idea of missions among the Black American churches.

Behind Crummell's social thought lay the oppressive reality of color caste, the offspring "of hereditary servitude." His grasp of the psychology of caste was superb. The effect of caste was dual: it led whites to believe mistakenly in their inherent superiority, and it led Blacks to the paralyzing belief in their own inferiority. So accustomed had whites become to wielding power that they remained convinced long after the collapse of the slave-plantation regime that "the natural place and destiny of the Black race" was "as *the* tillers of the soil." By the same token, they failed to recognize the existence of a class of talented and superior Black men. "And this," Crummell concluded, "is one of the signal signs of the deadly power of caste."

But it was with the effects of caste on the Black consciousness that Crummell was primarily concerned. Slavery and its effect on white attitudes, he told a group of Black workingmen in 1881, "have served to settle in the minds of large numbers of our race the idea that servitude *is* the normal condition of the Black man. Two centuries of service in this land has thoroughly driven this idea into the souls of thousands of our people; so that you can find numbers of Black men and women who really think that they themselves are inferior because they are Black; that the race was born for inferiority; and that they reach the highest state of honor when they become servants of white men." On every side, among the better off as well as the abject poor, Crummell saw the painful results of caste: the desire to deny race, the inability to organize to combat oppression, the unwillingness to defer material pleasures, the lack of a venturesome spirit, the feeling of helplessness, and the low level of aspiration.

True, the Black man did not cause these "painful and embarrassing circumstances," but he would have to initiate the steps to change them. Ever the believer in moral and mental improvement, Crummell confidently assured his congregation of middle-class Washington Blacks in 1875 that "character, my friends, is a grand, effective instrument which we are to use for the destruction of caste . . ."

Always the bouyant optimist, partly perhaps to combat the Black sense of inferiority, he entertained no doubt that the group had but to develop moral, social, and economic power, and "all the problems of caste, all the enigmas of prejudice, all unreasonable and all unreasoning repulsion, will be settled forever, though you were ten times blacker than midnight." Indeed Crummell seems to have concluded that the problem of caste was amenable to class solutions. His concern with changing the negative image of Blacks in the white and Black mind remained basic to the end. With customary optimism, he told the elite membership of the American Negro Academy in 1898: "You have already done a work that has told upon the American mind; and next you have awakened in the Race an ambition which, in some form, is sure to reproduce both mental and artistic organization in the future." For Crummell white attitude and Black self-concept were inextricably entwined.

The problems confronting Black people in the latter nineteenth century were many. In the minds of most, the means of solving these problems were work and education. Since Crummell had early reached this conclusion, and because of his reputation for scholarly rectitude, he was an important influence among the slowly expanding Black intelligentsia. For this practical Christian moralist, work and education were the vital means of cultivating character in a people so circumstanced as were Blacks. How, he asked, could Black labor—mainly unskilled and defenseless —increase its value and power? Most certainly, Black men must set out to acquire the skills and training, and if color prejudice froze them out of the trades, then they must organize to educate themselves. But if afterward the jobs were not there because of the insidious workings of the caste system, they could only fall back on the Horatio Alger rhetoric of the period. "But try; and try; and try again," he counseled some Black workingmen, "until you carve your way to the higher avenues to wealth and superiority." Indeed, with Crummellian honesty he admitted that he did not have a satisfactory answer to the labor question.

Crummell did much to construct the boundaries of the issue that came to a head at the turn of the century over the nature of the education best suited to the Black man's predicament. For him, as for most Black people, it was never a question of manual training or classical education. He had stressed both in his schools in Liberia. In the early years after his return to America, however, he tended to stress the need for manual training, not only for the masses but for the classes as well. For labor, he said in 1881, anticipating Booker T. Washington by a few years, is antecedent to culture and refinement.

But by the mid-1890s as the net of caste was being drawn tighter around Black people, industrial education became an *idée fixe* among more and more of the Black as well as white intelligentsia. Crummel, however, began to harbor reservations. He did not now turn about and repudiate industrial education, for more than the skills that it taught, what had always primarily recommended it to him was the moral discipline that supposedly inhered in it.

Rather, the issue was one of "disproportion and extravagance." The pendulum had swung too far in the direction of industrial training; it must now be made to swing back toward classical education. Otherwise, whence would come the leaders trained in the highest ideals of service and duty? From where the scholar-philanthropists who would solve such weighty problems as the economic status of Black people? Who would encourage the latent artistic genius, without which the race could not achieve cultural superiority?

But in Crummell's mind the debate over industrial and

classical education was a reflection of a larger issue. To this man unswervingly committed to the power of ideals, it seemed as the century drew to a close that those ideals were being imperiled by the tide of materialism sweeping over the country. Indeed, it seemed that within a few years, the stress among Black people on material accumulation had more than achieved its purpose. In an essay published posthumously in 1898, Crummell expressed satisfaction that the "acquisitive principle" had taken hold among Black people. However, he feared that in the scramble for its possession, property had become an end in itself, dissevered from the development and refinement of the "lofty motives" of character. "There is no elevation in this, no real progress, no substantial and abiding improvement!" he concluded. "Nothing but moral death!"

The answer to caste and the pervasive Black sense of inferiority was the development of a vigorous sense of Black peoplehood—or, if you prefer, nationality—through the planned development and use of Black resources. In 1883, in his lengthy response to a racist address by a white fellow clergyman within the Episcopal church, Crummell asserted that the millions of Blacks here "is not merely a people—it is a NATION." Crummell's own ripe sense of peoplehood drew upon his social experience in the Black community of his youth and in Liberia, where he preached a gospel of Christian Black nation-building and where he established an institution or two. It was strengthened, however, by a firm intellectual underpinning of scholarly Christian thought.

In Crummell's teleology, the beginning and the final cause was God. Love of God dictated that one should pattern his life after that of Christ, and since the labors of the Redeemer were constructive and restorative, so too must be the work of His followers. Each man, in the first instance, was responsible for the state of his own soul, but accompanying this concern—indeed, almost overriding it—was the responsibility to bring other souls to God. "The divine principle received in the soul, while it does not destroy personality," he wrote, "does lift us up and above the isolation of self . . . and into the brotherhood with the entire species of man." Linked to the brotherhood principle was his concept of gregariousness, the basic need of men to come together and organize for mutual aid, a common enough belief among Blacks in his youth.

Clearly, Crummell placed the claims of the group above the claims of the individual. Indeed, the individual achieved his grandest fulfillment in working for the commonweal. Not surprisingly, he locked horns on several occasions with his Washington neighbor, Frederick Douglass, who took a more libertarian stance, emphasizing personal freedom as an end in itself.

Like his onetime mentor, Beriah Green of Oneida Institute, Crummell believed that sanctification revealed itself in social service. "To talk of how we feel, or what we think concerning Christ, is an idle tale," preached the Christian activist. "No, my brethren, what our Lord desires is . . . religion made personal in the Christian life, act, word, conduct, and bearing of living disciples." One had to live his convictions, and he contributed most to the glory of God who joined with his fellows in concerted action for the world's good. This perfectionism remained the religious basis of Crummell's social thought.

Crummell was a scholar. He believed that the scholar must also be the philanthropist, that scholarship must be socially useful, and that the scholar-philanthropist should be active in the reconstruction of society. And so, following his permanent return to the United States in 1873, when the country was rededicating itself to the maintenance of color

caste, Crummell organized several noteworthy black institutions. In 1875 he founded St. Luke's Protestant Episcopal Church in Washington, D.C., and was pastor there
until 1895. Several years later, he formed the Union of
Colored Ministers of Washington, D.C., and as race relations worsened and the Black community there became
more fragmented, he called upon the Black clergy in 1892
to lead in establishing charitable institutions for the poor
and destitute of the race. In 1883, as the senior Black priest
in the Episcopal church, he called into being the first Black
caucus within the church to protest racism and repression.
And in 1897, the year before his death, he was instrumental
in founding and became the first president of the American
Negro Academy in Washington, D.C., established for the
double purpose of encouraging intellectual excellence
among Black people and countering the mounting volume
of racist propaganda against Black people in the caste-
ridden society. An idealist with an instinct for the practical,
Alexander Crummell practiced what he preached.

Related, too, to his principle of brotherhood was Crummell's belief in the widely held concept of peoples and societies as organisms. "It is evident, alike from nature and
revelation," he told his Episcopal church colleagues in
1888, "that the Almighty has created certain relations or
unities which are designed to absorb the personal, and to
mingle multitudinous units into organic wholes." The basic
social organism, of course, was the family. But if one's first
social responsibility was to one's family, it followed that
his next was to his race. For, as he said, employing the racial
thought of the time for *Black* purposes: "Races, like families, are the organisms and the ordinance of God; and race
feeling, like family feeling, is of divine origin . . . Indeed, a
race *is* a family." Crummell's belief in Black peoplehood,

therefore, rested not alone on hatred of color caste but as well on a mystical conception of race.

Because Christian brotherhood began nearest home, it did *not* follow that it ended there. In Crummell's mind, the "feeling of kinship" did not imply any limitation on "the brotherhood of the entire species." What he seems to have envisioned for the United States is what became known as a "pluralistic" society, with each racial and ethnic group retaining its integrity while participating and sharing in the governing of American institutions. This concept he had earlier applied to the international area, for nations too were parts of a larger organic whole. Liberia, he had argued, like other nations, had a duty to contribute to the world's progress. It was his belief that this contribution might well be moral. This idea was but part of a larger "Black Messianic" vision (Vincent Harding's apt term). Starting with the idea present in the early Black community that there was a providential meaning to the Black coming to America, Crummell over the years extended it to include the redemption of Africa by her westernized sons. He went on to formulate ideas which in the mind of a more subtle thinker like W. E. B. Du Bois became synthesized as the Black mission to redeem humanity from the harshness of white, Western civilization. Crummell's concern for the Black mission doubtless contributed to his anxiety in the 1890s over what seemed to him to be a growing absorption of the Black middle class with material wealth.

Founded on Christian doctrine, Crummell's ideal of Black peoplehood was strongly imbued with Protestant morality. Like individuals, no social organism—whether family, corporation, race, or nation—could grow without a clear idea of the Christian God and without the inward force of character, "the consummate flower of true religion."

To Crummell, a Christian social order—the only kind he would countenance—was one heavily impregnated with honesty, restraint, work, industrial enterprise, stable family life, and education and religion to discipline the intellect, inculcate the values of "thrift, order, acquisitiveness, virtue and manliness," and extend the sway of religious philanthropy. By these standards would he measure progress toward Black emancipation. For character thus defined must be the basis of "a grand moral revolution" that would achieve Black liberation, replacing the oppressiveness of inferiority with a manly sense of superiority. A work of decades, this revolution could only be achieved through the internal organization of Black people.

The question arises, did Crummell desire that Black people become simply (to use Nathan Hare's phrase) "Black Anglo-Saxons"? Because the social science thought of the time tended to equate or to confuse race and culture, an answer is perhaps more difficult to reach. For example, Crummell spoke of institutions as being "transmitted, in our blood to live, to the latest generations." Another component of this thought, however, was the belief in a hierarchy of social development that moved upward from savagery through barbarism to civilization. Unquestionably, for Crummell, British "civilization," with which he had long and intimate acquaintance, was the most advanced and the model for a "new and rising people" such as the Blacks. For it contained the proper mixture of liberalism and stern discipline which he believed essential for a people starting out in earnest along the path toward superiority.

But his intelligence and his sense of race pride would not allow him to rest there. He believed Blacks to be different from whites in more than skin color. Thus he characterized Black people as being gifted with vitality, humility, patience, endurance, religious susceptibility, hope, plasticity, and imitativeness. All of these characteristics, of course, whites had already attributed to Black people. But Crummell brought to them his own interpretation, attempting thereby to encourage a sense of race pride. For example, he asserted that the "quality of imitation," instead of reflecting, as some declared, a lack of originality, had led to Black elevation, for "the Negro, with a mobile and plastic nature, with a strong receptive faculty, seizes upon and makes over to himself, by imitation, the better qualities of others."

Indeed, the principle of imitation led Crummell to a more sophisticated concept of culture transmission. He noted that while the Black man assimiliated elements of the culture of the stronger group, he retained "his characteristic peculiarities." In addition to those "traits" mentioned above, these "peculiarities" included indigenous religious and artistic styles, a deep feeling of family, especially among Black women, and the redemptive quality of suffering. I have already alluded to his messianic idea. Suffice it to say, a number of these characteristics he viewed as carry-overs from Africa. For example, he seems to have entertained in embryo the idea of a Black aesthetic. Whether such insights were the traditional mouthings of missionaries or conclusions drawn from long residence in Africa or both is unclear.

All of these "traits" or "peculiarities"—call them what you will—Crummell viewed approvingly, for they were "natural" and so presumably divinely inspired. He did not, however, view them uncritically. For example, the emotional enthusiasm characteristic of many Black churches he found productive of good, but, he lectured his fellow Black clerics of Washington in 1892, it lacked the "fine and tender qualities which generate the assiduities of grand philanthropy." In the final analysis, what was missing were discipline, responsibility, economy, organization—fruits of character which he identified with Anglo-American culture. It seems that he wanted Black people to combine the efficiency of industrial society with the "characteristic peculiarities" of the Black idiom. This combination would lead to group progress and at the same time ensure racial integrity.

August Meier has pointed out that Black stress on economic and moral development was accompanied by a de-emphasis on political activity. It was over the political question that the philosophical differences between the two Black patriarchs, Crummell and Douglass, were made manifest. After his early years, Crummell seems never to have been enthusiastic about politics as a vehicle for Black advance. To be sure, he did not counsel Blacks to cease fighting for the ballot or protesting its denial. It was to whites that he stressed rights and justice since they were the ones doing the denying. To the Blacks he hammered away at duties and responsibilities. Frederick Douglass' slogan "Agitate! Agitate! Agitate!" was, therefore, to him a call for a wasteful expenditure of precious energy that should be directed inward toward the goals of mental and moral development. The achievement of these would ensure the attainment of all other forms of power.

To Douglass, the whole idea of "a nation within a nation" was absurd, though he had used the phrase on occasion. He emphasized rights and privileges. As Americans, Blacks were to enjoy the same privileges as all others. To Douglass, the struggle was for equal rights for Blacks as individuals, and this carried him beyond the Black community and out among the whites who indeed were doing the denying. The pressure for change must be brought directly against them rather than placing the onus of change on Black people or waiting for Crummell's long-term moral revolution—as desirable as it might be—to work itself out.

Crummell's negative view of politics, however, was a logical outcome of his larger system of idealistic belief. The *ideal* of democracy was good, for it sprang from "the idea of Christian brotherhood." Probably with the British system in mind, he argued that the best government was one that steered between "wild radicalism" on the one hand and the "iron bond of tyranny" on the other. Though not antidemocratic, he shared the elitist's distrust of politics as it was practiced in the United States in the late nineteenth century. His experience both here and in Liberia had led him to the view that politics was a school for demagogues who placed self-interest above the commonweal. "Friend Anderson," he reputedly said on his deathbed, "I have no fear of the future of the American Negro, for he belongs to a prolific, hardy and imitative race . . . but I do dread his leaders because most of them are unscrupulous, ambitious and ungodly men, who care nothing for the race but to use it simply to secure their own selfish and ungodly ends."

Of paramount concern to Crummell and others, as well as to the exclusive group that composed the American Negro Academy, was the question of Black leadership. Crummell once stated that "society everywhere advances only by the force and energy of minorities. It is the few who lift up and bear the burdens and give character to the many." Though he spoke mainly to the educated, it was especially at high school and college youth that he aimed his gospel of bourgeois peoplehood. "If the scholarly and enlightened colored men and women care not to devote themselves to these lowly but noble duties, to these humble but sacred conditions, what is the use of their schooling and enlightenment?" he asked a Black college audience rhetorically in 1885. From their thin but growing ranks, Crummell was confident, would come the intellectuals, teachers, preachers, and artists who would go into the fields, cabins, schools, colleges, and churches of Black America and by force of character and disciplined intelligence guide the mental and moral development of the masses.

There was in Crummell's concept of leadership—indeed in the whole concept of peoplehood—a marked element of elitism and missionary paternalism. The whole uplift philosophy smacked of it. The masses were to be elevated by their social superiors to levels of Anglo-American respectability, and the walls of caste would come tumbling down. This desire to elevate the race in order to lower the walls raises the question of whether in their expressed concern for the welfare of the masses the Black elite and the middle class have not in fact been more concerned with their own interests. The life of Alexander Crummell and his ideal of Black peoplehood, it seems to me, etch sharply for us the historic dilemma of the Black middle class. This group has derived its status and its idea of itself partly on the basis of white criteria and partly on the basis of its relationship with the mass of Black people. The impact of the caste and class values of the dominant society has been strong, and identification with poor blacks has been viewed as a negation of these values. This helps to explain Crummell's concern about the white man's failure to recognize the existence of the cultivated class of Blacks.

The national mythology adheres to an open society. There is the belief that conformity to the values of work and moral rectitude will lead to "success." Crummell had internalized these values and had been rewarded. The system could thus be made to work for others, if not as individuals, certainly as a collectivity. He expressed the view well: "Along the lines of my own personal life I have seen the gracious intrusions of a most merciful providence. Every disaster has been surmounted and eclipsed by some saving

and inspiring interposition. It is not merely a personal experience. It is a wider truth. It is a fact and a principle
which pertains to the large and struggling race to which we
belong." In Crummell's statement we see the need to confirm the validity of one's life.

It may be that the greater the distance, social and
otherwise, from the Black masses, the easier it has been for
many Blacks to accept white definitions of them. In Crummell's case, the separation may have been accentuated by
the cloistered habits of the scholar surrounded by shelves
of books filled with wrong-headed ideas. That he was thoroughly familiar with the advanced Anglo-American thought
of his age on race is evident from his own writings. That he
accepted some of it—perhaps far too much—is equally clear.
It should also be remembered, however, that he rebutted
much of it and refashioned some other of it for his own
purposes.

But we have not yet done with the class issue, for it
was further complicated by divisions within the Black middle class itself. One manifestation of the growing differentiation of American life at the end of the century was the
appearance of a new middle class in the Black as well as
the white community. One might, then, view Crummell's
reaction to what he regarded as the overemphasis of the
middle class on property accumulation as the long-established gentry's exasperation with the antics of the nouveaux.
A few others—Du Bois among them—of the exclusive membership of the American Negro Academy shared this elitist
concern. The reason Crummell should have thought the
issues of caste amenable to class solutions now becomes
clearer: he was dealing with a class as well as a race problem.

There was also present in Crummell's concept of Black
leadership a strong component of Christian service, the

"answering heart of man responding to the beating heart of his brother." He was saved from the worst effects of elitism by his Christian faith—his profound belief in brotherhood and his boundless optimism. Whatever its shortcomings, the early Black community had developed a body of tradition that, among other things, valued service to the most oppressed of the race. In the midst of the fragmentation of life in the latter nineteenth century, and the increasing proscription of Black people, Crummell was concerned with strengthening that tradition of service. In the final analysis the two elements—bourgeois self-concern and a commitment to service—formed a symbiotic relationship in his mind. That this was so is demonstrated in the following revealing passage:

> And then the "poor, forsaken ones," in the lanes and alleys and cellars of the great cities; in remote villages and hamlets; on old plantations which their fathers' blood has moistened from generation to generation; ignorant, unkempt, dirty, animal-like, repulsive, and half heathen—brutal and degraded; in some States, tens and thousands, not slaves according to the letter of the law, but the tools and *serfs* of would-be oppressors; stand by THEM until the school-master and preacher reach them as well as us; and the noble Christian civilization of the land transforms their features and their forms, and changes their rude huts into homes of beauty; and lifts them up into such grand superiority, that no one in the land will associate the word "Negro" with inferiority and degradation; but the whole land, yea, the whole world shall look upon them by-and-by, multitudinous in their brooding, clustered masses, "redeemed, regenerated, disenthralled," and exclaim, "Black, but comely!" But, while they are low, degraded, miserable, almost beastly, don't forget that you are colored men, as well as they; "your brothers' keepers."

Through it all, two things remained clear: who the oppressor was and who the oppressed, and the vast gulf between democratic rhetoric and the realities of Black life in this land.

After such a sketch as this, one is inevitably drawn to the question, what does it all mean? How do we assess a man whom W. E. B. Du Bois eulogized as a "noble soul" who in another age "might have sat among the elders of the land in purple-bordered toga . . ."? True, Crummell seems to have influenced a number of important Black people, notably Du Bois himself, and he founded a handful of organizations that outlived him. St. Luke's Episcopal Church still thrives. Important as these things are, it seems to me, they are not, to use Crummell's language, the most abiding things.

The first of these, I suggest, is his optimism. Near the end of his life he remarked: "One large truth I wish to put before you, namely, that standing now more than three score years and ten, in age; the scars of bitter caste still abiding, I am nevertheless, a most positive OPTIMIST." If such a faith appears to us today incredibly naive, we have only to recall that he lived in an age that firmly believed in the idea of progress. The emancipation of millions of slaves confirmed him in his optimism. And we might well ask, Is such a faith all that misplaced even in our own time? Despite his scholar's reliance on history, Crummell was essentially future-oriented. However much one might criticize it, Crummell at least *had* a vision of the future, without which we seem destined to remain prisoners of an oppressive past and present. Faith that one can influence the course of events, as Crummell's life illustrates, can steel the will to resist injustice. Moreover, even as he regarded the Black poor as beastly, he had no doubt that one day Black would be beautiful. Finally, his faith, born of his deep spiritual commitment to brotherhood, that people of different backgrounds could somehow live together, is not altogether outmoded.

The second thing of lasting significance in assessing the meaning of Alexander Crummell is that we remember that he was a scholar, and that with more insight and integrity than most of his contemporaries he pursued the truth. There is something heroic about this lonely Black man who spent a long life wending his way through a scholarship filled with lies and half-truths about Blacks to arrive at his own Black truth. However one views his version of the truth, there can be no doubt that Crummell was a pioneer in the establishment of a Black tradition of scholarship. One might, of course, cite others; Edward Wilmot Blyden and George Washington Williams come to mind. But it seems to me that there was no consistent body of scholarly Black thought before Crummell. To his reflections of more than a half-century on the universal Black predicament, he brought a scholarship that we today would label interdisciplinary, combining at the very least, religion, history, sociology, psychology, and philosophy. It is no coincidence that the scholarly and versatile Du Bois could liken him to the savants of another time and place.

Crummell was a systematic thinker who, like his friend and former colleague Blyden, attempted a synthesis of Africa and Afro-America. For him the destiny of Blacks everywhere was tied to their fate anywhere. They were bound together by ties of kinship and social experience that transcended class and geographic boundaries. This was the view of many of those early "Africans in America." The lineaments of his Liberian nationalism were the same as those of his Black peoplehood here. In this sense, one might say that he desired to Afro-Americanize Africa. Actually, when Crummell declared American Blacks to be a nation, he was stating a hope. It was something to strive for. Crummell's ideal of Black peoplehood was a response not only to color caste; it was a response also to the growing fragmentation of late-nineteenth-century American life and conformed to the need for a renewed sense of community. Crummell helped supply that need to a small but growing circle of concerned Black people.

It is doubtful, however, that Crummell contributed much to an accurate knowledge of the African people and African societies. His mind was simply too imbued with Western missionary ideas to expand much beyond such false, value-laden categories as paganism and barbarism. His views, ironically, may have contributed heavily to the negative image of Africa in the Black middle-class mind at the turn of the century. At the same time, he seems to have had an influence on the continuing interest among Black churches and within his own denomination in establishing Christian missions in Africa.

There is a final enduring importance to all of this. What Lerone Bennett, Jr., said of the leaders of "the Black pioneer period," "that . . . at least they held these ideas sincerely and lived them instead of merely mouthing them," applies with equal or greater force to Alexander Crummell. There is a unity of life and thought here which, even if one does not always approve, invites admiration. He preached "a Christianity with bones and muscles," and he lived a life that led one close friend to describe him as "a Christian athlete." For what were leaders—scholar-philanthropists—if not models for the followers. If one is called to missionary labors, one works actively to redeem souls; if one is to be a scholar, one directs his intellect toward the highest standards of excellence. Such was Alexander Crummell.

# V. Prelude to Disaster

## An Analysis of the Racial Policies of Boer and British Settlers in Africa Before 1910

by Okon Edet Uya

### I

Few words in the international vocabulary engender more opprobrium and initiate more hatred than apartheid. For all its euphemistic equivalents of "separate development," "parallel development," and "along their lines develop- ment," apartheid is synonymous with racism, tyranny, op- pression, and fear. Because it insists on an ethnic minority ruling over a majority, the basic prerequisite for its success- ful implementation is rigid control of people, and the gov- ernment has fashioned appropriate instruments for such control.

Because it was not until 1948 that the South African government officially institutionalized apartheid as a pol- icy, there is the tendency to forget that apartheid as prac- ticed since 1948 has deep roots in South African history. There is also the tendency to regard racial policies of the South African government as the codification of a peculiar Afrikaner syndrome. In fact, some tend to compare the "militant and decidedly oppressive attitude of the Boers" with the "more enlightened liberal policy" of the British

settlers in South Africa.[1] In this paper the author argues
that although the rhetoric of race relations may tend to indicate a breakdown along the British-Afrikaner line, where
the strategic and economic interests of the various groups
were deeply involved, the racial policies of the British
settlers in South Africa were not appreciably different from
those of the Afrikaner before 1910.

## II

Before the term "apartheid" came into use in 1948, the
racial policies and attitudes of the Boers in South Africa
can be viewed as expressions of Afrikaner nationalism. Afrikaner nationalism expressed itself in three forms: an ag-
gressive and destructive and at best oppressive attitude
toward the aborigines of South Africa, the Africans, whom
the Boers considered to be outside the pale of salvation and
doomed to extinction or perpetual control; the hostile attitude toward the British, who, in the formative years, appeared to be the disturbers of the peace and the "divinely
ordained" order of things; an increasing self-awareness
that South Africa was "a fatherland for the Afrikaner people." These mutually inclusive elements constitute Afrikaner nationalism.

The origin of Afrikaner nationalism has been a subject of historical controversy among scholars. Professor
Floris Van Jaarsveld of the University of South Africa, the
best-known authority on the subject, argues that Afrikaner
nationalism was born in the last quarter of the nineteenth
century. Before this time, he maintains, the Boers in South
Africa acted independently of each other and "had not
become nationally minded before the seventies and eight-
ies of the 19th century, and did not develop any assertive
nationalism before 1881." The Afrikaners, Jaarsveld fur-

ther states, "lacked an historical awareness of themselves and the cohesive force that could supply inner unity, and provide them with a common future, past and present."[2] In another study, Jaarsveld ascribes the origins of Afrikaner nationalism to the period 1868 to 1881.[3]

It would appear, however, that Jaarsveld is dealing with the last element mentioned above in the development of Afrikaner nationalism. For a feeling of unity among the Boers in South Africa, as expressed in anti-African, anti-British utterances and actions, predated the nineteenth century. These are important ingredients of Afrikaner nationalism. As Jaarsveld admits, there is in Afrikaner nationalism "a sense of having been called and chosen," and this feeling has deeper roots in South African history than Jaarsveld would have us believe.[4] Admittedly, the term "Afrikaner" did not come into use until after the Great Trek, and even then it was applied to the Boers who trekked from the Cape to the interior. Essentially, however, this was a mere change of nomenclature calculated to emphasize to the Boers their distinctive mission. Obviously the "feeling of belonging" among the Boers had deep-rooted links with the spiritual, social, political, and economic circumstances that contributed to the evolution of the Afrikaner people in South Africa.

There is also no agreement as to whether this peculiar feeling of belonging was imported from Europe or grew on South African soil. It is difficult to establish whether or not sentiments similar to those of the early Pilgrims in the New England colonies in colonial America animated the Dutch colonists who settled at the Cape in 1652 and later. It would appear, however, that if such feelings were present initially, they could not have been very strong. The Dutch East Indian Company that established the colony, possibly because of the numerical inferiority of its members, was apparently anxious to maintain good relations with the indigenous peoples and believed that intermarriage would be one way of ensuring this. Thus, the surgeon of the little colony was given a promotion when he married a christian Hottentot woman called Eva. A wedding party was held in the commander's house. Although the Dutch settlers tended to despise the Hottentots because of their very simple material culture, it would appear that this was basically a matter of culture and religion rather than race. Freed black slaves acquired burgher status and lived on familiar social terms with their white fellow farmers; the children of mixed marriages were readily accepted as members of the small white society. Distinctions there certainly were, but these appeared to have been between "Christians and barbarians." Indeed, for two centuries, the Dutch Reformed church tried to uphold the principles of the oneness of all Christians. "The issue was not what a man's color was, but whether he was a member of the Christian church."[5]

These attitudes, however, began to change in succeeding years. Driven by the restrictive posture of the company and the lure of better economic opportunities in the interior, the Boers began to move inland and came to live in isolation among Hottentots. The fear of losing contact with their own group led to an increased sense of racial solidarity. The Boer farmer came to find himself in a position of authority over a mixed group of servants, many of whom were not accustomed to the work which the farmer required of them. Isolated from other farmers, the Boer farmer could only hope to enforce his commands if he and his servants accepted his position of authority without question. In such a situation, a myth of racial superiority appeared a necessity for survival.

The introduction of slave labor on a large scale after

1716, and the almost total elimination of a white laboring class, produced a sharp stratification of society along the lines of color. "A reluctance to work" became a way of life for the Boers, with taboos and religious and social sanctions to justify it. Thus, the foundation of a society of Black servants and white masters was established. Finally, the struggle against the Bushmen, and later the Bantu, would have a generally brutalizing effect. The value of non-European lives was lowered in the eyes of the Boers.

Soon the original attitude of ignoring racial differences, except where they were accompanied by cultural and religious contrasts, was replaced by an ever-increasing race consciousness. Africans came to be looked upon more as living instruments than as persons—an important ingredient in Afrikaner nationalism. Religion itself was now interpreted to sanctify the status quo. Contrary to the official synods of the church, most simple farmers came to believe that discrimination between the races was the will of God. In 1703, for example, the church council of Drakenstein wrote to the Convocation of Amsterdam on the subject of Hottentots whom it wished to convert "so that the children of Ham would not longer be servants or bondsmen." The convocation expressed approval and the hope that "one day God would lift the curse from the generation of Ham."[6] The Boers henceforth saw themselves as God's chosen people to bring civilization to the "barbarians" in South Africa. To fulfill this sacred mission, they felt themselves called upon to maintain their purity of blood, their religion and culture. Thus, by 1685, intermarriage was forbidden officially between whites and African women. Increasingly, too, the Boers came to apply to themselves literally the contents of the Old Testament. The nonwhites came to be identified not only with the children of Ham but also with the Canaanites of the Promised Land. They referred to the in-

digenous population as "Naatsies" (nations without laws)
and sometimes as Philistines.[7]

By the end of the eighteenth century, therefore, the
Boer settlers had come to look upon themselves as "humans
and Christians" and upon the Africans as "heathens." By
believing in this, General Janssens observed that by the
turn of the century, the Boers permitted themselves "everything." "Whenever they needed more land they moved
the frontier and took what they wanted." The "common
Europeans," he continued, had "become gentlemen and
they desired to be well attended upon." "Accustomed to
call for slaves from his youth onwards," observed a young
Dutch seaman, the Afrikaner "believes that he is elevated
above all and may only be obeyed."[8]

This master-servant society which emphasized to the
Boer his self-importance and higher status appeared to be
threatened by the establishment of British overlordship in
1806. By this time, the Hottentots and Bushmen who had
served as a buffer between the Boers and the Bantu had
been largely eliminated, having been either absorbed into
Bantu groups or forced to enter the service of the whites.
At the commencement of this second British period, the
government at the Cape tended to regard the Hottentot
stations as schools of idleness keeping useful labor off the
market. The government was also determined to govern
and to exercise legal control over labor regulations. Thus,
in 1809, in a series of regulations, the status of the Hottentots was clearly defined: they must have a fixed address,
and could not travel from one station to another without
a pass. Failure to conform to these stipulations would make
them liable to arrest. In 1812 a further ordinance was issued giving white farmers the right to apprentice Hottentot children for ten years.

Though these regulations were clearly biased in favor

of the Boer farmers, since they virtually forced the Hottentots to enter the service of the Boers, they also recognized
the legal status of the Hottentots. Disagreements between
the master and the servant were to be subject to legal
arbitration. This was anathema to the Boers, as it contradicted their attitude that the Hottentot was subhuman and
therefore outside the protection of the law. Consequently,
attempts to enforce the regulation by the Black Circuit
Court were forcefully resisted and triggered off several
uprisings by the Boers. These uprisings fizzled out without
serious fighting, but not before the ringleaders were captured and seven of them publicly hanged at Slachtere Nek.
By this action, the British government served notice, to the
consternation of the Boers, that it meant to rule effectively.
The Black Circuit Court and other labor reforms, J. A. L.
Agar-Hamilton has argued, "would be approved by the
economist but they upset the frontiersman's conception of
the universe."[9]

The momentum of reform continued in the following
years. The philanthropic movement was gathering force
for the final struggle over emancipation of slaves, and missionaries addressed a flood of complaints to a receptive
public in Britain on behalf of the Hottentot protégé. In
1826, Dr. John Philip published his *Researches in South
Africa,* and though he was successfully sued for libel in
the Cape, the book had an immense effect in England. By
skillfully combining an appeal to morality against the near
slavery of the Hottentots with arguments based on current
laissez-faire orthodoxy, the book arrested the sympathy
of many segments of the British public in behalf of the
Hottentots. This liberal posture by individuals and government in Britain culminated in the passage of the 50th
Ordinance in 1828 and the abolition of slavery in South
Africa in 1834. The former removed all restrictions to which

the Hottentots were subject and placed them and other free colored persons on a basis of legal equality with the whites. The latter provided for compensated emancipation of slaves, adding that after a period of apprenticeship to their former masters, slaves would come under the provisions of the 50th Ordinance and enjoy legal equality with their erstwhile masters.

These two laws were direct affronts to the Boer idea of good society and the sense of mission. Even though the financial losses involved were galling, the social consequences were simply unbearable to the Boers. Not surprisingly, complaints about these acts featured prominently in the next dramatic episode in the history of South Africa —the Great Trek. Arna Steenkamp listed one of the causes of the trek as "the equalization of nonwhites with the Christians." She considered this to be "in conflict with the laws of God and with natural distinctions of origin and belief."[10] To the Boers, therefore, British policy was an unwelcome interference with "the divinely established social order." It amounted to a revolution in the legal ethos of society and constituted a direct affront to the Boers' sense of racial superiority. In addition to this, the government extended this "equalization" policy to the eastern frontier. The farmers on the frontier came to the conclusion that the British were backing the Africans against them. The result was the Great Trek, which was viewed largely as a necessary step to ensure their safe existence for the future beyond the borders of the colony and for the retention of their philosophy and way of life.[11]

Undoubtedly, the Great Trek, from one point of view, can be regarded simply as an acceleration of the process of white expansion under the pressure of land hunger which had been going on from the earliest days of the Cape Colony. The Boers resented British taxation and land policies.

The British government appeared to them to act like an insatiable and impersonal grinding machine. From this point of view, it could be regarded as a reaction to better economic conditions. The trek, however, was more than this. Unlike the advancing settlers of earlier times who had always taken the frontier with them, the Great Trek Boers appeared to be engaged in a conscious movement of secession. They left the colony determined to shake off British rule forever and to establish a community of their own to be governed on their own principles. Economic grievances they certainly had, but their greatest grievance was their hatred for the principle of racial equality that the British had come to represent. Louis Trechardt, one of the leaders of the trek, told the Portuguese on the coast that his chief reason for trekking had been British emancipation of the slaves. Willen Jacobu Pretorious gave this as "the chief incentive" to the trek. In his manifesto calling for the trek, Piet Retief announced to his party that "whilst we will take care that no one shall be held in a state of slavery, it is our determination to maintain such regulations as may suppress crime and preserve proper relations between master and servant."[12] From this point of view, therefore, the Great Trek was the first dramatic expression of the anti-African, anti-British elements in Afrikaner nationalism.[13]

The Great Trek produced a scattering of Afrikaners all over the interior and led to the establishment of the two Boer republics, the Transvaal and the Orange Free State. The formation of these republics consolidated Afrikaner national consciousness. But it also brought them greater dangers. The farther they penetrated into the interior, the more numerous their African "enemies" became. Moreover, the trek into the interior, which was calculated to put the Boers outside the British protective, though unwelcome umbrella, actually brought them more and more within the orbit of British strategic interests in South Africa. The trekkers were to fight against these two traditional "enemies" well into the twentieth century. The more tenaciously they fought against these forces, the more determined they were to maintain their independence.

The trek of the Boers into the African hinterland triggered many military engagements with their African neighbors to the interior, the Bantu, who were equally determined to preserve their hegemony. Famous among these were Vegkep, Kapain, and Blood River.[14] The "treachery" often displayed by the Africans in encounters like that of Dingaan at Blood River further "confirmed" the Afrikaner opinion that Africans were "a people without a law" and unable to abide by the "decorum" governing the relations between peoples. The Boers were urged on by a firm belief in their mission. Retief felt that he was summoned by God to the leadership to ensure Boers' establishment in the interior, and believed that "God in His compassion will bring us in safety to our appointed destination." Other well-known leaders of the trek all expressed the hope that somewhere in the interior the trekkers would become "a nation and there an abode would be prepared for the whole Afrikaner race." "Since such things flow from the Almighty," one of them confidently proclaimed, "if it be His will and pleasure, we shall there become a nation and live to His honour." To them, their difficulties and trials were a mere title page to a glorious volume. They looked upon themselves as an instrument in God's hand to put an end to "plunder, murder, and violence in the interior and promote the extension of Christian civilization among many thousands whose existence heretofore has been rooted in darkness."[15]

Having dressed themselves in this messianic garment,

the Boers continued to view the Africans as natural subjects for colonization. The corollary of Christian love was
absent in the Old Testament theology which formed the
cornerstone of the beliefs of the "very religious" Afrikaners. Rather, they viewed themselves as the Israelites of old
and South Africa as the Promised Land. When, for example, Commandant P. E. Sheltz had subdued the chief
Sechele during the 1850s, he declared that he had acted in
the matter according to the divine law which had been
entrusted to Joshua.[16] The Transvaal constitution of 1858
contained a basic principle that "the people desire to permit no equality between colored people and the white inhabitants of the country, either in church or state." The
fundamental postulate of Boer native policy, one historian
of that subject has concluded, "was that the native was
inferior, [and] absolutely precluded from receiving political privilege."[17] This, of course, remains to this day a tenet
of Afrikaner nationalism.

The trouble with the Africans, however, represented
just one aspect of the crisis the Boers faced in the interior.
Of equal importance for the consolidation of Afrikaner
nationalism was the attempt by the British to undo the
South Africa that had come into being during the period
1830 to 1954 and substitute for it a politically united country under the British flag. The discovery of minerals in
the interior and the quickening pace of the scramble made
this movement more urgent. It is not the purpose here to
tell the story of how Britain, through a policy of hesitancy
and vacillation, conditioned by the changing climate of
opinion in Britain and South Africa, came to lose control
over South African developments.[18]

At all events, the Boer desire for independence ran
counter to British strategic and imperial considerations for
South Africa. The result was a series of Anglo-Boer con-

frontations which had three points of climax: the Transvaal War (1880-81), the abortive Jameson Raid (1896), and the Anglo-Boer War (1899-1902). In these conflicts, Boer nationalism and British imperialism tugged against each other for the control of South Africa. The Boers succeeded in the first two, but lost the field to the British in the last, though political gains soon blotted out their military humiliation. Significantly, these crises promoted and corresponded to high points of Afrikaner nationalism.

In 1877 there were accusations by the British and complaints that the Transvaal Republic had not established law and order in the interior and that the nonwhites had been enslaved and oppressed. President Kruger of the republic and Piet Joubert, one of his supporters, wrote to Michael Hicks Beach denying these allegations. The Transvaal, they maintained, "was a flourishing and self-supporting state, a source of strength and security to neighboring European settlements and a center from which Christianity and civilization was spreading rapidly into central Africa."[19]

Up to this point, however, the Afrikaners had shown little disposition for acting in concert against their British and African "enemies." Each of the republics had pursued its policy independently of each other, though the results tended to be the same. At the outbreak of the Transvaal War, however, sentiments were expressed which revealed an increasing awareness by Afrikaners of the necessity to act together in the common danger. President Kruger uttered a statement which was said to be typical of the prevalent mood of the time. "Whether we conquer or perish," he is quoted to have said, "freedom will emerge in Africa . . . as surely as the sun rises out of the morning clouds. And then, from the Zambesi to Simon's Bay, it will be a case of Africa for the Afrikaner." During that war, many Afrikaners turned their thoughts to their mission, which was always to them a great source of inspiration and courage. A Free Stater, for example, exclaimed: "I consider and believe that this land is the land ordained by God since time began in which we should wage our final fight for freedom." A group of Transvaalers proclaimed that "God rules and is with us. It is His will that we should unite as one nation and create a united South Africa that is free of British authority."[20] These were typical of the image of the future implanted in the minds of many Afrikaners. Clearly, it was the antithesis of that envisaged by English-speaking South Africans—a united South Africa under the British flag. "The preservation of their independence," Lord De Villiers observed of the Boers at the time, "is a sacred mission."[21]

The mood was particularly prominent after the influx of outlanders to the Rand following the discovery of minerals there in 1886. The Afrikaners were continually warned not to abjure their origin. They must not be cast into the melting pot in such a way that their identity and character were submerged. When Dr. Jameson led the abortive raid into the Transvaal in 1896, Afrikaners in all parts of South Africa reacted in unison to demand justice for Kruger's republic. Dr. Jan Mansvelt, a prominent leader, expressed his faith in the future of the Afrikaner people. "After so much strife and suffering to win and develop this lovely and richly endowed land," he declared, he could not believe "that Providence had destined the Afrikaners to disappear from history without a trace and to give way to others."[22]

This new found sense of unity was promoted by the Anglo-Boer War of 1899-1902. During the war, Lord Salisbury of Britain was quoted as saying that the Afrikaner people should not exist. Kruger's rejoinder to this was that God had said "such a people shall exist." To many Afrikaners the war was indeed the final act in the drama of what they called a "century of wrongs." It was the logical culmination of the posture of the British regarding developments in South Africa. In 1902 the Reverend S. J. du Toit maintained that it was the English, who through "the blows of her lash," had aroused a spirit of fraternity and patriotism among the Boers. Defeat in the battle did not diminish this almost fatalistic belief in their mission. In 1906 President Steyn urged the Afrikaners to bear their burdens "until the Almighty achieves His purpose with His people."[23]

By the end of the Boer War, therefore, the Great Trek, their establishment in the republics, clashes with the Bantu and the British resulting in loss of lives and land, had all combined to give rise to a feeling of solidarity among the emigrant farmers. The military successes against the Bantu confirmed their belief in their superiority over the Africans, while confrontations with the British brought home to them the fact that they were involved in a common destiny.

These, however, were largely negative responses to situations of crises. As time went on, the Afrikaners also realized that they had to develop a positive aspect to their nationalism—cultural nationalism and political parties—for the translation of their ideals and principles into practical policies.

"The great constructive policy of South Africa," J. C. Smuts, an Afrikaner nationalist, declared in the 1880s, had "for its objective the stimulation of those forces which make for progress."[24] In Afrikaner thinking, such "stimulation" implied conscious interpretation of the Afrikaner past to act as a spur to the then brewing sense of nationalism, and a rejection of the current history which did not show the Afrikaner in "sufficiently good light." History thus became, for the Afrikaners, a means of arousing the nationalistic

sentiments of the young by accenting the heroic acts of
their forefathers and reciting "a catalogue of British oppres-
sions" to justify present posture.

From 1876, Boer popular writers and historians set
out to write just such nationalistic history denouncing existing history as inadequate in the process. "British History
and Cape History," they declared, were calculated to ex-
tinguish any idea of Boer nationality. It was high time, one
writer maintained, "that our children should be made acquainted at school in their own language with the *true* history of the land of their birth. For too long have we received stones in lieu of bread, snakes instead of fish, and
scorpions rather than eggs." One farmer asked if the time
had not come "for some capable persons to write a concise
history of our country for us ordinary people, so that there
may be an end to the dissemination of such one-sided histories as those of Hall, Wilmot and Chase that libel the
Afrikaner." The Reverend S. J. du Toit pointed out that the
poor Boer was always shown in a bad light and complained
that the British books contained "twisted and partisan pre-
sentations and reflected narrow-minded prejudices."[25]
Afrikaner self-discovery directed attention to history, and
the indignation aroused led to a flood of books purporting
to present "accurate facts"—facts designed to foster self-
esteem and pride.

The first to appear, *The History of Our Country in the
Language of Our People* (1887), testified to a wounded self-
esteem. As opposed to the existing works that viewed
"everything through English spectacles," the new book set
out to tell things as "they really were." "Tell the truth," it
declared in the preface, "correct the lie and again bring to
notice the deeds of our forefathers." Boer leaders of the
Great Trek were depicted as great warring heroes who
sacrificed themselves so that their children might enjoy the

fruits of their suffering. The Great Trek itself was viewed as an occurrence through divine intervention so that branches from the mother stock might take root in their appointed positions in the interior. In this way, the British were merely instruments in God's hand to awaken the Boers to their historic mission, which they appeared to have forgotten. The engagements with the Bantu were played up, and the breach of faith by African chiefs bent on arresting the expansion of the Boer frontiers given prominence, to justify racist attitudes. The aim of the book was clearly didactic, and the spirit and mood nationalistic. The purpose was "to acquaint our children from their childhood of the trials and sufferings of their forefathers in this land where foreigners now seek to tread us under feet." Significantly, but not surprisingly, the book was very well received. One correspondent declared that it was "surely the best way to develop our sense of nationhood and to strengthen the harmonious bonds of friendship among the people." A Free Stater appealed to the editors to "please see that thousands of copies of your little history book are printed so that every true Afrikaner can have one in his possession and so that all may know what South Africa cost their forefathers."[26] This publication became an inspiration for other works written in the same vein.

In the pages of these new "histories" the Afrikaner people tried to sustain themselves and maintain the justice of an irrational cause. History thus became a bulwark of nationalistic politics and provided a fresh impulse for the political front. The more the Afrikaner saw and identified himself with the heroic past, the more powerful were the stimuli for the struggle of the day.

The Afrikaner spirit was also nurtured by religious and cultural organizations. Gradually, the Dutch Reformed church came to be the center for the propagation and ventilation of nationalistic impulses. An Afrikaner clergyman saw the Transvaal War in the following terms: "Behold the armies of the Lord of salvation; we are like Israel of old —before us lay the Red Sea, behind us was the Egyptian host and on either side of us were lofty mountains. We could but look up and cry to God and He heard our voice."[27] In 1882 the Reverend du Toit declared in a sermon that the English were their chastisers. The Society of True Afrikaners was formed in 1875, and the Journal *Die Patriot*, founded in 1875, fanned the Afrikaners' sense of injustice and inspired them to be true to the *volk*.

Meanwhile, Afrikaners were developing political vehicles for the expression of their grievances and the consolidation of their nationalism. In 1879 the Afrikaner Bond was formed at the Cape. The party propagated the idea that there ought to be a free and independent South Africa and chose as its rallying cry, "Africa for the Afrikaners." "Just think from whom we Afrikaners are descended," the party declared in 1886. "We are largely descendants of poor refugees on account of their beliefs from European countries . . . Just think how our forefathers fought and struggled to ensure their freedom and our freedom, and how many of them had to sacrifice their lives."[28] In the Transvaal, the Het Volk, and in the Orange River Colony, the Orangie Unie, were organized in succeeding years. The wars with the British, which aroused a feeling of affliction, common home, origin, and destiny, drew the *volk* toward a common future and one in which the political ideal expressed was that of a united South Africa under Afrikaner control. The Milner reconstruction and Anglicization program after the Boer War acted as a political cement to these feelings of nationalism.[29] To preserve their language and custom "uncontaminated," the Boers established a movement for Christian National Education which founded rival schools to those established by Milner. In the years immediately after the war, Boer political parties, the Het Volk in the Transvaal, Orangie Unie in the Orange River Colony, and the Pro-Boer Afrikaner Bond at the Cape, won at the polls.

By about 1910, therefore, Afrikaner nationalism had triumphed over all the opposing forces in South Africa. The Africans had been put in the position reserved for them in the Afrikaner "divinely inspired" social, political, and economic order. There had been political successes in all three Boer states. The Afrikaners, now had a language, a history, a realization of their sense of mission, a pride in self, and, above all, the right political atmosphere to translate their principles and beliefs into political realities.

### III

Although British posture in the Cape Province and toward the Boer republics was sufficiently tainted with humanitarianism to justify the liberal label often attached to British policies in South Africa, the actions of British settlers in Natal tend to show that, where fundamental issues were involved, the attitude of British settlers toward Africans was not very different from that of the Boers. Natal was the most English of all the white settlements in South Africa. A few English settlers had been there as early as 1824 but they were largely ignored by the British and Cape governments until the Great Trek Boers defeated the Zulu and established the Republic of Natalia in 1838. Alarmed by the threat now posed to control of the interior trade and the possibility of an independent hostile community establishing itself on the Indian Ocean so near to the Cape, the British government annexed Natal in 1843. The action was justified as imperial altruism calculated to stop Boer cruelty to the Africans in the area.[30]

Great Britain now had a colony in which the "native question" loomed large. The departure of the Boers left the English settlers in the vast majority among the whites in Natal. Here, then, was the opportunity to test the newly emergent humanitarian impulse in practice. A burst of fervor had brought manumission of slaves; British naval vessels patrolled the African coasts to assist in suppressing the nefarious slave trade. In South Africa itself the Hottentots at the Cape had been identified as objects of British philanthropy and accordingly protected by the 50th Ordinance. Could this same spirit be extended to the newly acquired Natal? The British government and the settlers were called upon to answer this question in several ways— the land question, the labor problem, taxation, and the granting of the franchise to Africans. Three views, varying in the intensity of their differences over time and issue, were brought to bear on these problems. These were the policies expressed by the government in London, the view expressed by the colonists in Natal, and those of the British missionaries who sought to proselytize the Africans. Of these, the second will be emphasized, since it was the colonists' policies that ultimately prevailed and since these views represent the only true variable of the three—the others being applied in the other areas of the British imperial system in South Africa.

In 1841 the Natalia Volksraad had advocated the establishment of a system of reserves as being "highly necessary for the safety of the community."[31] Despite the fact that the most important reason professed for the annexation of Natal was dismay with the native policy of the Boers, a native commission, appointed in 1846, in turn supported the establishment of a number of locations, and this policy was supported by the British government in the person of the lieutenant governor of the colony.[32]

The chief architect and most obdurate advocate of this policy was Theophilus Shepstone, who was appointed "Diplomatic Agent to the Native Tribes."[33] Shepstone believed in what he called "differentiation," or what is today euphemistically termed "separate development." As a result, the commission recommended that the Natal authorities "adapt their decisions to the usages and customs of the Native Law where such accommodation can be effected without violating the requirements of justice."[34]

Opinion was unanimous in the colony that, as the colonial secretary of Natal phrased it, "a distinct line be established between the different races of Her Majesty's subjects."[35] Of course the argument was advanced that such a policy would find favor with the Africans, who would realize the wisdom and benevolence of the government's acts. The colony was relieved when Shepstone, who then, as later, exercised great personal influence over his wards, was able to shepherd them into their reserves.

The Natal colonists found two aspects of British native policy particularly inimical. They considered the size of the locations to be too large, and objected to the policy of granting titles in the locations on an ethnic or sectional rather than individual basis. Their arguments and activities on these two questions underscored the moral bankruptcy and essential hypocrisy of their position.

When the location system was completed in 1864, about 10 per cent of Natal's land area was included in it. Furthermore, the sea areas were among the poorest in the country agriculturally. A land commissioner testified to the 1852-53 Natal Native Commission that "I have satisfied myself that not more than about 2000 acres [of the 450,000 then established] ever has been, or, humanly speaking, ever could be available for cultivation."[36]

The irony of the settlers' contention lies in the fact that

in the years immediately preceding their most violent objections, other land in the colony had been uselessly frittered away. To prevent an exodus of the Boers from Natal, Sir Harry Smith, governor of the Cape Colony, had sought to maintain their good will by giving them the traditional 6,000-acre areas for farms. In justification, Smith claimed his action would "conduce to the restoration of happiness to thousands, tend to the preservation of the Christian community . . . and the production . . . of harmony and peace."[37] The Boers accepted the proffered gift, sold it to speculators, and moved across the Drakensberg Mountains into the Transvaal. Thereby the land became unavailable as well as unproductive, and the "thousands" to whom happiness was restored were reduced to a few speculators. Later, from 1857 to 1860, another 1,360,000 acres were given to less than 300 colonists in an effort to attract immigrants. Inevitably the colony, in its largesse, began to find itself running out of land, and it therefore became increasingly difficult to attract settlers. By 1874 six million acres—or thrice the acreage encompassed within the locations—were in the possession of less than 8,000 whites. This unhappy situation only intensified the outcry over the size of the locations.[38]

Initially, however, the colonists found a willing ally in Benjamin Pine, lieutenant governor from 1850 to 1855, and they found further solace in the attitude of Sir George Grey, governor of the Cape and high commissioner. Pine attacked the locations as "immense" and "vast" and claimed the Africans were "consolidating themselves" in them.[39] Grey likewise denounced the "enormous" and "inconvenient" locations, but more in terms of their effects on the labor supply.[40] Pine convened a new native commission in 1852. This body castigated its predecessor as having failed "chiefly owing to the size of the locations it recommended, which led it to trespass largely on the private rights of proprietors of farms, and [more significantly] dried up the source whereby an abundant and continuous supply of Kaffir labour for wages might have been procured."[41]

Despite this, the protest of the colonists had no visible effect on the location system, at least in structure. Nevertheless, from 1864 to 1953 the area of the locations increased only 2 per cent while their populations increased fivefold.[42] The majority of the inhabitants were thus forced to leave the locations.

Although not codified until 1864, the practice from the inception of the location system had been to invest title in the ethnic groups or chiefs rather than individuals. The Natal colonists, in their desire to "improve and regenerate" their Black brothers, found this practice abhorrent.[43] Furthermore, the legislative council feared that "tribal tenures" would "increase the dangers to the colony" and result in a "preponderating influence by the missionaries." Pine was amenable to their plaints, but his successor, John Scott, refused to succumb to their blandishments. Scott considered the colonists' schemes as "impracticable, harsh and hazardous." He proposed, in turn, "giving tribal or sectional titles vested in responsible trustees," the policy then practiced. Responding to Scott's contumacy, the legislative council petitioned the colonial secretary to persuade Scott "either to desist from carrying out his proposed policy . . . or to remove him from a field of operations where his views differ so entirely from those of the inhabitants of the Colony."[44] The Colonial Office chose to support Scott's position in this controversy. Perhaps thinking it indelicate because of his office, Scott had refrained from referring to the colonists' proposals as worse than "harsh," but the home government was less loath to recognize the colonists' purposes. "The granting of individual titles," wrote a colonial undersecretary, "is simply impracticable at the present moment and were it so, the White colonists would soon get all the land from the Natives for a mere song."[45] In consequence of these suspicions the Native Trust was established in 1864. All the lands in the locations were alienated to this trust, and neither ethnic nor individual titles were provided for.[46] Nonetheless, in 1882 the attorney general of Natal could report that "no land has been transferred . . . to any Natives in 'individual and unfettered freeholds'."[47] In this respect the colonists were thwarted in their efforts to secure the Africans' land, but on the other hand, as we have noted, the extent of this land remained almost constant after 1864.

Colonists arriving in Natal expected to find an abundant labor supply eagerly awaiting them. This belief was fostered by the propaganda issued by the various associations formed to stimulate immigration to the colony.[48] These expectations, however fatuous, were not fulfilled. From the very establishment of the colony the settlers had complained of the inadequacy and uncertainty of the African labor supply. The preference of many settlers for Australia, even before the gold strikes there, was attributed by many to this assumed shortage.[49] In the formation of the locations the settlers found their bête noire. Objections were raised to locations "whose fertility [sic] is such as to offer irresistible temptation to indolence."[50] Even Theophilus Shepstone commented, "the Natives lack neither land nor cattle in such quantities that their desires go no further than the elementary ones of sufficient to eat and time to sleep."[51]

As early as 1854 it was suggested that the presence of "patient and industrious foreign workers" would be a salutary example to "the indolent Kaffirs," and in 1860 the first of several thousand Indian migrant workers were introduced into the colony.[52] In the 1870s Natal made an arrangement to receive freed slaves from East Africa, but most of these continued on to the mines of the Cape. It would seem, then, that there existed a unanimous and informed opinion on the matter of a labor shortage. In fact, this was not the case. A traveler in 1850 commented on the ability of farmers to obtain labor. Edmund Morewood, the founder of the sugar industry in Natal, regarded the labor shortage as a "bugbear" and concluded that the "cry of 'want of labour' is almost exclusively raised by persons who either cannot afford to employ servants or who expect unreasonable returns for small pay and cheap food."[53]

The Natal colonists were wont to refer invariably to "labour for wages," thereby implying a contractual, regularized, and conscientious arrangement between employer and employee. But regrettably, this would be taking too much for granted. A contemporary observer commented on the situation in 1850 thus:

> The sense of right and justice, which always dominates the mind of the British workman, impelled him to offer the Native wages, food and shelter, according to the custom of the country. This he found upon inquiry to be defined in nautical terms as "Monkey's allowance, more kicks than ha'pence," for the Boers had left a legacy of unbelief in the propriety or fitness of the Native to acquire or receive wages—he should be thankful for the Baas's protection and shelter, with such scraps and cast off things as might fall his lot. If he was especially good, it was generally understood that at the end of a year's faithful service he might receive a cow, or even a cow and a calf worth 25s or 30s, but it too frequently happened that at the year's end the Baas found it inconvenient to part with either servant or beast. If the native dared to remonstrate, his life was made burdensome, with the gratifying result that he retired from active service to his Native bush, leaving the cow behind

him, for to take the cow, allotted to him, meant pursuit and possible death.[54]

Finally, there is evidence that the British colonists used the labor available to them as wantonly and inefficiently as they did the land. In testifying before the Native Commission in 1852 a district magistrate observed:

> On a farm he [the African] does almost everything. He herds the cattle, milks the cows, churns the butter, loads it on the wagon, the oxen of which he inspans and leads. He cuts wood and thatch, he digs *sluits* and makes bricks, and reaps the harvest; and in the house he invariably cooks. There is little I ever see a farmer do but ride about the country. In the town there are some cases in which the Kaffir labour is employed to a ridiculous extent; for in what quarter of the globe would adult males be found performing the offices of nurses to infants and children, or as laundresses of female apparel?[55]

This proclivity, reminiscent of the Old South in America, had reached such alarming proportions in 1873 that the lieutenant governor, Anthony Musgrove, felt constrained to comment on the situation as it then stood. He deplored the lack of self-reliance among the whites in Natal and compared their industry unfavorably with that of the Africans.[56] His remarks implied that scarcely twenty years after their formation, the locations had proven inadequate to accommodate the increasing population. It is not unlikely, however, that the whites would still have regarded them as "vast" and "enormous."

It is apparent that an extravagant expenditure of the available work force combined with a disdain for work and an honest approach in their dealings with the Africans on the part of the colonists caused what seemed to be a severe labor shortage. But a great deal of this problem was artificially induced and terminable at any given moment that the colonists saw fit to deal with it with a modicum of common sense and integrity.

If the land and labor policies in Natal fell somewhat short of providing equality or even dignity to the Africans, the government strove manfully to correct this by granting them the civic privilege of paying taxes. In considering means to fortify the colony's initially poor financial position, Shepstone recommended the imposition of a hut tax in 1849.[57] Shepstone saw this tax as serving social as well as revenue purposes. He felt it had the "further recommendation of discouraging poligamy [sic]," since, of course, each wife normally had an establishment of her own. Shepstone recommended a tax of five shillings *per annum*, but the council decided a figure of seven shillings would be more reasonable. The revenues from this tax soon reached £10,500 annually, or one-third of the total revenue of the colony. Colonists were aware of the crucial importance of this tax. "The country was insolvent," rhapsodized the *Natal Independent*, "and we owe its salvation to our Black brethren." Shepstone agreed, in observing that "the Native population of Natal contributes to the revenue annually a sum equal, at least, to that necessary to maintain the whole fixed establishment of the Colony for the government of the Whites as well as themselves."[58]

Satisfied with the success of their experiment, many in Natal delighted in claiming that the colony had "taught her elder sister [i.e., the Cape Colony] a step in the right direction" regarding taxation. And in fact, the Colonial Office, in recommending such a tax for the Cape, alluded specifically to that in Natal.[59] Nominally, the payment of a tax is expected to result in some tangible benefits. By 1854 the

hut tax had yielded over £35,000 but only £1,500 was being spent annually on native affairs. Lieutenant Governor
Pine rationalized this by asserting that "it would be easy
to show that a third of the general expenditures of the Colony is rendered necessary by the presence of a large Native
population."⁶⁰ Hence, revenues were being expended not
for, but because of, the African. To obviate this misuse of
funds, the charter, granted in 1856 when Natal became a
separate colony, carefully stipulated that £5,000 a year be
"reserved" exclusively for native purposes. Furthermore,
responsibility for this sum was retained by the lieutenant
governor in council. Even though the hut tax alone was already yielding over twice that amount, this £5,000 reser-
vation was vociferously denounced by the colonists and
became the issue that was most obnoxious to them. The colonists, over a period of thirty-five years, strenuously and
continuously sought to have it abolished or surrendered to
the tender mercies of the legislative council. In fact, it is
likely that Natal might have been granted responsible government before 1893 had the British government been assured of Natal's good faith in this matter.

During the entire existence of the tax under the colonial government a constant theme was the willingness
with which the Africans paid it. "The tax was generally
paid with cheerfulness and the justice of its imposition
properly understood," Pine assured his superior.⁶¹ High
Commissioner Smith concurred, stating that the tax "had
been paid willingly and has produced no discontent."⁶²
John Robinson, the first premier of Natal, claimed that

Taxation imposes little burden. The paternal government
which provides them with security and labor, asks in return a payment so small that the produce of a few fowls,
or the wages of a small boy, will suffice to meet it.⁶³

However, there is considerable evidence to contradict this comforting viewpoint. The doubling of the hut tax in 1875 led to "considerable overcrowding" which would hardly have occurred had the tax not proven burdensome.[64] Pine himself admitted that one reason for the initial response to the hut tax was that most felt it would be a single rather than an annual tax. Exemptions were granted for natives having but one wife and living in "European-style" dwellings, but the number of these exemptions dropped by almost half from 1883 to 1898 and presumably continued to decline thereafter.

But the hut tax was scarcely the only form of taxation imposed on the Africans. In 1876 there was a five-pound marriage tax—a potent stimulus to monogamy, one would suspect. Then there was a dog tax, an impost on beads, and finally, in 1905, a poll tax. Any poll tax, being uniform, will bear most heavily on lower income groups or, in this case most obviously, the Africans. From 1893 to 1910 the percentage of income devoted to paying taxes among the Africans increased and was already (in 1893) greater than the percentage of the whites' income.[65]

This evidence is persuasive that the types of taxation imposed on the Africans by the Natal authorities were both discriminatory and burdensome, and were so perceived by both taxer and taxed.

The colonists often congratulated themselves on their efficient use of Africans as sources of revenue. The extent of their sophistry illustrates that they were probably aware of real implications. Yet in the matter of granting the franchise they quite surpassed themselves in artful rationalization. In 1853 a "nonracial" franchise had been established in the Cape. Largely at the insistence of Dutch agricultural interests, who did not want to be subordinated to the wealthier English-speaking urbanites, the property qualification was set at twenty-five pounds rather than at a higher figure also proposed.[66] The charter granted to Natal in 1856 contained a property qualification of fifty pounds. This was designed to exclude not only the Africans but also the "half-pay or retired officers of the Army and Navy" who "swarmed" into the colony.[67] The charter provided some provision for ultimately granting the franchise to Africans and was not explicitly racially oriented. Nine years later, however, an act was passed which could scarcely be characterized as anything but an effort to effectually and permanently deny the franchise to the Africans. No colonist was really satisfied with the 1856 provisions. Even Theophilus Shepstone felt constrained to assure the whites that "not a native in the colony has had anything whatever to do with the return of any hon. member of this house."[68]

It is peculiarly ironic that at this period, when the colonists were agitating for individual ownership of land, ostensibly on the basis that it would "improve" and "regenerate" the African, they simultaneously wished to deprive him of the right to exercise the franchise. Such actions betrayed the basic cynicism which motivated the colonists' activities. The import of the act of 1865 was to add further barriers to the property qualifications established in 1856. That the act proved effective may be measured by the responses to it by those interested in the Africans' welfare and, more practically, by the number of Africans on the voting rolls. The London Aborigines Protection Society complained in 1875 that the act was "so loaded with technicalities and the process [for enfranchisement] . . . is made so complex that in practice it has become a dead letter ever since it was passed."[69] The society's assessment remained valid long after. In 1904, 2 Africans, 7 Griquas, and 103 Coloured possessed the franchise.[70] Although Harriette Colenso and others advocated some extension of the franchise,

if only because "the mere willingness to acknowledge . . .
equal rights would indicate such a departure from the
'sjambok and rifle theory' . . . as would mean that the main
root of the [native] difficulty or problem had ceased to
exist," these were scarcely the arguments to influence the
Natalian politicians, particularly after responsible government had been acquired and nothing whatever was done.[71]
In fact the Native Commission of 1906-7 recommended that
the disenfranchised Africans not be allowed representation
among the unofficial members of the council, claiming that
"not one of the many [sic] educated and exempted Natives
. . . suggested that one of their own race should be their
Member. Their readiness to be represented by selection
from nominations made on their behalf was an exhibition
of moderation, political wisdom and confidence in the
European which is highly commendable."[72] In fine, the attitude of the colonists on this franchise question was probably accurately summarized by John Robinson who observed that the disfranchisement of Africans "is so obvious
a necessity . . . that it hardly calls for comment." He echoed
a widespread belief among the colonists when he added
that there was "every reason to fear that they would be the
prey of party or interested agitation," and significantly concluded, "the natives, moreover, would be the great majority."[73]

And so, during the colonial period, the Africans were
effectively and totally, if scarcely forthrightly, barred from
securing the franchise.

In creating the location system Shepstone was apparently sincere in believing it would further the interests of
the Africans as he saw them. The system was initially designed as a flexible one, necessary for the times but subject

to modification in the future.[74] This was emphasized in a circular sent to all district magistrates in 1850:

> Whilst humanity, and especially the injunctions of our religion, compel us to recognize in the Natives the capability of being elevated to perfect equality, social and political, with the White man, yet it is as untrue as it would be unwise to say that the Native is even now in this position, or that he is in his present state capable of enjoying or even understanding the civil and political rights of the White man.
>
> Her Majesty's Government has most wisely recognized and acted upon these principles by providing a form of Government for the Natives in the District, which, while adapted to their present position, *is capable of being so modified as to advance their progress toward a higher and better civilisation.*[75]

In spite of the blatant, if not uncommon, ethnocentrism expressed in this circular, it manifests an apparent willingness to allow the position of the Africans in Natal to improve. Yet, as we have seen, these sentiments, once enunciated, were soon forgotten. The Shepstone system stagnated to the point of ossification. Shepstone himself seemed to become more accommodated to the views of the colonists in terms of the labor problem and the franchise.[76] The culmination of this transmogrification was seen in Shepstone's policies toward the Africans after he was appointed administrator of the newly annexed Transvaal in 1877.

A boundary dispute had festered for several years between the South African Republic and the Zulu. Despite the ruling of a boundary commission awarding much of the disputed territory to the Zulu, Shepstone, in his own words, "tore to tatters" this decision and secured the annexation of the entire disputed territory to the Transvaal.[77] Those who advocate a cyclical theory of history would find much comfort in these actions. Thirty years before, the Cape government had attempted to secure the good will of the Boers at the expense of the Africans and failed. In 1878 the same policy produced the same results. Additionally, the policies of 1878 instrumentally precipitated the Zulu War.

In 1873 the Langalibalele Rebellion occurred in Natal. The Natalians' reaction to this very minor insurrection is illustrative of their attitude toward their "native problem." Once the rebellion was suppressed, the reserve on which Langalibalele and his people had dwelt was reduced in size by about one-quarter and the lands sold "on condition that they should be occupied by resident White men."[78] The Amahluli and Putili clans, who participated in the revolt, were "utterly dispersed and their land and cattle confiscated."[79] Langalibalele himself was hurriedly and improperly tried by a tribunal which included two members whose sons had been killed in the campaign. He was banished, but not far enough to suit many. The reaction in Great Britain was critical of the measures adopted by the Natal authorities and Benjamin Pine, serving his second tour in Natal, was recalled and pensioned off. The Natal colonists were fond of Pine and supported his policies then as they had twenty years previously. Robinson later defended Pine's actions as having been "recognized as those of a far-seeing and high-minded statesman."[80] Sir Garnet Wolseley was sent out to Natal as a special commissioner to institute reforms to curb the influence of the colonists. His supporters were referred to as "howling humanitarian fanatics," but his critics were soon silenced, for Wolseley "came to reform and remained converted."[81] Soon he was complaining that

"England with her humanitarian notions of governing bar-barians is really responsible for the danger now existing in Natal."[82] Consequently, no useful reforms were carried out, and in fact the resentment of the Natalians at what they considered unwarranted British interference may well have served to reinforce their attitudes.

In 1893 responsible government was finally granted to Natal. Great Britain had long resisted agitation for this in Natal, primarily because she feared the consequences of an unrestrained native policy in the colony. Surprisingly, when responsible government was granted, the only safeguard of African interests included was a clause stipulating that £10,000 be appropriated annually for "native purposes."[83]

British and American missionaries had been resident among the Zulu before the annexation of Natal to the British Empire. One might innocently suspect that they served as buffers in seeking to modify and blunt the policies and pro-posals of the colonists, but in fact very few seem to have opposed these measures and most found it relatively easy to accommodate themselves to them. For example, the mis-sionaries emphatically favored "detribalization," expecting that thereby the Africans could be more easily prosely-tized.[84] The Reverend William C. Holden, a Methodist mis-sionary, composed a tract in 1851 devoted to the "labour problem." He was chagrined that many settlers were leav-ing the colony "in despair and disgust" because they had failed to find a labor force plentiful enough to supply their wants.[85] He castigated the British government for "handing the Natives over to irreclaimable heathenism and bar-barism" by establishing the locations. He opposed poly-gamy because "thousands" of Africans were "supported in independent idleness by their wives" and hence presum-ably not inclined to "labour for wages." He proclaimed:

> Let the *people not become actual possessors of the land by
> gift,* but let them purchase it "at a reasonable rate" or bet-
> ter yet let them gather together where they would be *de-
> pendent for their subsistence upon their labour in the ser-
> vice* of the White Man.[86]

Aldin Grout, an American missionary, favored individual
tenure. Daniel Lindley, another American missionary,
seems to have served his flock with more fidelity to the principles of Christianity.[87] But the American Missionary
Society declared:

> The British are incomparably more humane and enlight-
> ened in their Native policy than any other political Power
> in South Africa. . . . We desire to declare . . . our apprecia-
> tion of the administration of law and order on behalf
> of the black races under the aegis of freedom-loving
> Britain.[88]

In sum, there is little evidence to indicate that the missionaries in Natal and Zululand made substantial or sus-
tained efforts to do more than nominally proselytize the
Africans and introduce them to the road to salvation
through the medium of laboring for the white settlers.

## IV

Thus, by the time of the Unification Convention the
racial policies of the white settlers in South Africa, with the
possible exception of the Cape Province, were very similar.
For the Boer republics, the real significance of unification
was, as historian J. D. Omar-Cooper has rightly observed,
that "it occurred at a time when the Boer War and its after-
math had greatly increased the forces of conservative
Afrikaner nationalism, so that the spirit of the frontier was
able to triumph over the more flexible outlook of the
Cape."[89] Significantly, too, the position taken by Frederick
John Moor, prime minister and the leading Natal delegate

to the convention, was unquestionably the least uncompromising of the four delegations on the native question. Responding to a suggestion from Sir Percy Fitzpatrick of the Transvaal that a truly nonracial franchise clause be embodied in the proposed constitution, Moore replied that

> In his opinion the white and Black races in South Africa could never be amalgamated. The history of the world proved that the Black man was incapable of civilisation and the evidences were to be found throughout South Africa. Almost every race in the world could point to its stages of civilisation but what traces of Black civilisation could Africa produce though the native people had been brought into contact with civilisation for ages? What again was the experiences of the United States of America? It would be the same in South Africa if the same policy were adopted and the American Negro had gone back to the condition of his ancestors in the jungle. The natives were incapable of civilisation because they were incapable of sustained effort. He for one wanted a settlement of this question now and he *felt he could speak for the Natal people*.[90]

Little wonder then that at the convention the Natal delegation was as opposed to the extension of the liberal Cape franchise as their Afrikaner countrymen in the Boer Republics. No doubt the routes taken by the various European settlers in dealing with the "African problem" in South Africa were different, but they led to the same practical result. The South Africa that came into being after 1910 was clearly the making of whites in South Africa, irrespective of their national origins. These events proved a truism—that in matters of great importance, blood is always thicker than water. This might also explain South Africa's confidence today in boldly maintaining its anachronistic system in the face of the "wind of change" hopefully still blowing over the African continent. Without international white

support, South Africa cannot maintain its apartheid system
of oppression and victimization.

## NOTES

[1] Colin Legum, "Nationalism in South Africa," in Anene and Brown,
ed., *Africa in the Nineteenth and Twentieth Centuries* (Ibadan
University Press, 1966), p. 421.

[2] F. A. Van Jaarsveld, *The Afrikaner Interpretation of South African History* (Cape Town, 1964), p. 42.

[3] Jaarsveld, *The Awakening of Afrikaner Nationalism, 1868-1881*
(Cape Town, 1961).

[4] Legum, "Nationalism in South Africa," p. 421.

[5] See, for example, I. Schapara, *The Khoisian Peoples of South
Africa* (Routledge, 1930); S. D. Neumark, *Economic Influences
on the South African Frontier, 1652-1886* (Stanford, 1957); I. D.
MacCrone, *Race Attitudes in South Africa* (1937), p. 41.

[6] Cited in Jaarsveld, *Afrikaner Interpretation,* p. 6.

[7] Henry Gibbs, *Background to Bitterness* (London, 1954), pp. 13-
50.

[8] Cited by Legum, "Nationalism in South Africa," p. 421.

[9] J. A. L. Agar-Hamilton, *The Native Policy of the Voortrekkers*
(Cape Town, 1928), p. 9.

[10] Jaarsveld, *Afrikaner Interpretation,* p. 7.

[11] See, for example, Okon Edet Uya, "The Great Trek as an Expression of Afrikaner Nationalism," *The Historia* (University of Ibadan, June 1966); P. J. Joubert et al., *A Century of Injustice* (Baltimore, 1899); Francis R. Statham, *Blacks, Boers and British*
(London, 1881); Lee Roy Hooker, *Afrikanders: A Century of
Dutch-English Feud in South Africa* (Chicago, 1900); Gibbs,
*Background.*

[12] Cited in Gibbs, *Background,* pp. 52-3.

[13] For analysis of the Great Trek, see the following: Eric Walker,
*The Great Trek* (A & C Black, 1960); Leo Marquand, *The Story
of South Africa* (London, 1963); W. M. Macmillan, *Bantu, Boer
and Briton* (Oxford, 1930).

14 Hugh Marshall Hole's *The Passing of the Black Kings* (Glasgow, 1932), though dated, is still very valuable for this subject.

15 Cited in Jaarsveld, *Afrikaner Interpretation*, pp. 15-17.

16 See William Kistner, *The Anti-Slavery Agitation Against the Transvaal Republic, 1850-1868* (Cape Town, 1952), II, p. 211.

17 Agar-Hamilton, *Native Policy*, p. 88.

18 See, for example, De Kiewiet, *History of South Africa: Social and Economic* (Oxford, 1941), *British Colonial Policy and the South African Republics, 1848-72* (Longmans, 1929), and *The Imperial Factor in South African History* (Cambridge, 1937); also William J. Leyds, *The Transvaal Surrounded* (London, 1919).

19 Cited in Jaarsveld, *Afrikaner Interpretation*, p. 18.

20 Ibid., pp. 19-20.

21 J. S. Marais, *The Fall of Kruger's Republic* (London, 1961), pp. 331-32.

22 Jaarsveld, *Afrikaner Interpretation*, p. 20.

23 Ibid., pp. 21-29.

24 Cited in Gibbs, *Background*, p. 140.

25 Jaarsveld, *Afrikaner Interpretation*, pp. 38-40.

26 Ibid., p. 40.

27 Ibid., p. 11.

28 Cited in Legum, "Nationalism in South Africa," p. 426.

29 For a discussion of Milner's policy, which actually amounted to cultural imperialism, see the following: E. Crankshaw, *The Forsaken Idea: A Study of Viscount Milner* (New York, 1952); W. Worsfold, *Reconstruction of the New Colonies Under Lord Milner* (London, 1942); Eric Walker, *Lord Milner and South Africa* (British Academy Proceedings, 1942).

30 For a full discussion of the debate over the occupation of Natal, see the following: G. W. Eybers, ed., *Select Constitutional Documents Illustrating South African History, 1795-1910* (London, 1918), pp. 146-48; John S. Galbraith, *Reluctant Empire: British Policy on the South Frontier, 1834-1854* (Berkeley: University of California Press, 1963).

31 J. R. Sullivan, *The Native Policy of Sir Theophilus Shepstone* (Johannesburg, 1928), p. 17.

32 A. E. du Toit, "The Cape Frontier: A Study of Native Policy with Special Reference to the Years 1847-1856," *Argiefsjaarboek*, Vol. I (1954), p. 92; E. H. Brooks and Colin de B. Webb, *A History of Natal* (Pietermaritzburg, 1965), pp. 58-59. In Natal, unlike the other South African provinces, the term "location" referred to rural reserves as well as urban villages.

33 Sullivan, *Native Policy*, p. 22.

34 E. H. Brooks and Hurwitz, *The Native Reserves of Natal* (Capetown, 1957), p. 4.

35 Daniel Moodie to Natal Land Board, August 22, 1848, in British Parliamentary Papers, 1850, XXXVIII, p. 69.

36 Quoted in Alan Hattersley, *Portrait of a Colony: The Story of Natal* (Cambridge, 1940), p. 217.

37 H. G. W. Smith, *The Autobiography of Sir Harry Smith*, edited by G. C. M. Smith (2 volumes, London, 1901), II, p. 235.

38 De Kiewiet, *Imperial Factor*, pp. 189-90.

39 Parliamentary Papers, 1852-1853, LXII, C. 1697, *Further Correspondence Relating to the Settlement of Natal*, pp. 22-23.

40 Du Toit, "Cape Frontier," p. 112.

41 Quoted in Brooks and Hurwitz, *Native Reserves*, p. 69.

42 Ibid., pp. 11, 22-23.

43 John Robinson, *A Life Time in South Africa, Being the Recollections of the First Premier of Natal* (London, 1900), p. 146.

44 Parliamentary Papers, 1862, XXXVI, 293, pp. 7-10.

45 Minute of S. G. Borrow of November 29, 1861, quoted in du Toit, "Cape Frontier," p. 277.

46 E. H. Brooks, *The History of the Native Policy in South Africa From 1830 to the Present Day* (Pretoria, 1927), pp. 357-358.

47 M. G. Gallwey to Earl Kimberley, Colonial Secretary, March 7, 1882, in Parliamentary Papers, 1883, XLVIII, C. 3796, p. 32.

48 See, for example, H. M. Robertson, "The 1849 Settlers in Natal," *South African Journal of Economics*, XVII (1949), 277; Alan Hattersley, *The British Settlement in Natal* (Cambridge, 1950), p. 228.

49 Alan Hattersley, "Inter-Colony Migration in Early Victorian Times," *South African Journal of Economics*, XXIV (1956), p. 281.

[50] *Natal Mercury,* July 25, 1851, quoted in Hattersley, *British Settlement,* p. 237.

[51] Quoted in Brooks and Hurwitz, *Native Reserves,* p. 4.

[52] *Natal Mercury,* quoted in Young, "Native Policy," p. 251.

[53] *Natal Mercury,* January 18, 1853, quoted in Alan Hattersley, *Further Annals of Natal* (Pietermaritzburg, 1940), pp. 89-90. See also R. F. Osborn, Valian Harvest, *The Founding of the South African Sugar Industry,* 1848-1956 (Durban, 1964), p. 53.

[54] George Russell, *The History of Old Durban and Reminiscences of an Emigrant of 1850* (Durban, 1899), pp. 103-4.

[55] Edwin W. Smith, *The Life and Times of Daniel Lindley, 1801-1880, Missionary to the Zulus, Pastor of the Voortrekkers,* (New York, 1952), p. 213.

[56] Musgrave to Kimberley, January 6, 1873, quoted in de Kiewiet, *Imperial Factor,* pp. 202-03.

[57] Proposal of Shepstone to Natal Legislative Council, June 18, 1849, in Parliamentary Papers, 1850, XXXVIII, C. 1292, p. 65.

[58] Quoted in de Kiewiet, *Imperial Factor,* p. 194.

[59] Earl Grey to Sir Harry Smith, January 7, 1851, Parliamentary Papers, 1851, XXXVII, C. 457, p. 38.

[60] Young, "Native Policy," pp. 236-237.

[61] Pine to Grey, September 28, 1850, Parliamentary Papers, 1850, XXXVIII, C. 1292, p. 16.

[62] Smith to Grey, February 26, 1850, in ibid., p. 164.

[63] Robinson, *Life Time,* p. 317.

[64] Zbigniew A. Konczacki, *Public Finance and Economic Development of Natal, 1893-1910* (Durham, N. C., 1967), p. 141.

[65] Ibid., pp. 147-155.

[66] Stanley Trapido, "The Development of the Cape Franchise Qualification of 1853," *Journal of African History,* Volume V, No. I (1964), pp. 46-54.

[67] Stanley Trapido, "Natal's Non-Racial Franchise of 1856," *African Studies,* XXII (1963), p. 24.

[68] *Natal Witness,* July 27, 1860, quoted in Trapido, "Natal's Non-Racial Franchise," p. 26.

[69] Aborigines Protection Society to Colonial Secretary, November 4, 1875, in Parliamentary Papers, 1876, LII, C. 1401, p. 88.

70 Du Toit, "Frontier Policy," p. 291.

71 Shula Marks, "Harriette Colenso and the Zulus, 1874-1913," *Journal of African History*, Volume IV, No. 3 (1963), p. 406.

72 Cited in Parliamentary Papers, 1908, LXXII, C. 3889, pp. 21-22.

73 Robinson, *Life Time*, pp. 308-09.

74 See, for instance, the various works of du Toit and Brooks cited in this study.

75 Memorandum of October 29, 1950, quoted in Brooks, *Native Policy*, p. 51. Emphasis added.

76 Brooks and Webb, *History of Natal*, pp. 76-77.

77 Sir James Silverwright quoting Shepstone to John X. Merriman, November 9, 1878, in Phyllis Lewson, ed., *Selections from the Correspondence of John X. Merriman, 1870-1890* (Cape Town, 1960), p. 58.

78 Wolseley to Carnarvon, May 17, 1875, Parliamentary Papers, 1875, LII, C. 1342, p. 30; and Carnarvon to Wolseley, July 3, 1875, ibid., pp. 34-35.

79 De Kiewiet, *Imperial Factor*, p. 38.

80 Robinson, *Life Time*, pp. 126-127.

81 De Kiewiet, *Imperial Factor*, pp. 43, 46.

82 Wolseley to Carnarvon, June 12, 1875, quoted in ibid., p. 45.

83 Brooks and Webb, *History of Natal*, pp. 174-178, 188.

84 De Kiewiet, *Imperial Factor*, p. 37.

85 W. C. Holden, *A History of the Colony of Natal* (London, 1855), p. 178.

86 Ibid., pp. 186-87.

87 Smith, *Daniel Lindley*, p. 256.

88 Quoted in Robinson, *Life Time*, pp. 323-24.

89 J. D. Omar-Cooper, "South Africa from the Great Trek to Unification," in Anene and Brown, ed., *Africa in the Nineteenth and Twentieth Centuries*, p. 410.

90 Quoted in Edgar H. Walton, *The Inner History of the National Convention of South Africa* (Cape Town, 1912), pp. 123-24.

# VI. Two Bronze Titans

## *Frederick Douglass and William Edward Burghardt Du Bois*

by Rayford W. Logan

I am honored by the invitation from the Frederick Douglass Memorial Lecture Committee of Morgan State College
to address this assembly.[†] Since the committee authorized
me to select the topic, I have chosen "Two Bronze Titans:
Frederick Douglass and William Edward Burghardt Du
Bois."

　　Both the time and place are significantly appropriate.
The life of Douglass is well known to you by your reading
of Professor Benjamin Quarles' scholarly biography, *Frederick Douglass*, as well as some of his other writings. I hope
that many of you are taking advantage of Professor Ellen
Irene Diggs' long association with Dr. Du Bois. She, Dr.
Du Bois' widow, Mrs. Shirley Graham Du Bois, and I probably are better qualified to discuss his life and works than
any living person. I hasten to add that, in a scientific sense,
I did not know him. He erected a kind of invisible barrier
which said, in effect: "So far, but no farther." I did not
know Douglass, of course, for he died a little less than two
years before I was born. I shall, therefore, speak less briefly
about Douglass than about Du Bois.

　　[†]This Frederick Douglass Memorial Lecture was delivered on
February 22, 1971, at Morgan State College.

137

Douglass was born in mid-February 1817, Du Bois on February 23, 1868. Their lives are indelible parts of the history of Baltimore. At the age of ten Douglass was brought to live with the Auld family in Baltimore where Mrs. Auld taught him to read and seemed to say to him: "Look up, child, don't be afraid." When Mrs. Auld's husband put an end to what he probably considered something dangerous —and he was right—Douglass had as his curbstone teachers several white boys. In Baltimore, too, were planted the seeds for his great career as an abolitionist when at the age of thirteen he read and then reread in *The Columbian Orator* the speeches of some of England's great statesmen. From the speeches particularly of Richard Brinsley Butler Sheridan, he later wrote, "I got a bold and powerful denunciation of oppression and a most brilliant vindication of the rights of man." It was the Baltimore *American* and other Baltimore newspapers that made him understand the bitterness of slaveholders and their sympathizers against abolition. After three years, 1833 to 1836, in what he called "the country," he returned to Baltimore. While working as an apprentice in a shipyard he was brutally beaten by some white apprentices. He wrote later in his *Life and Times* that his left eye was knocked nearly out of its socket. His ensuing comments are relevant today. "The slaveholders," he wrote, "with a craftiness peculiar to themselves, by encouraging the enmity of the poor laboring white man against the blacks, succeeded in making the said white man almost as much a slave as the black slave himself." Although Douglass had become a skilled caulker before he escaped from slavery in Baltimore in 1838, he encountered similar discrimination by white workers in New Bedford, Massachusetts. They told him that "every white man would leave the ship in her unfinished condition if I struck a blow at my trade upon her." He was forced to work as a laborer.

Substituting some employers of today for the slaveholders and many trade unions of today for the white workers provides a devastating parallel. I believe also that discrimination by white against Negro workers was a prime reason for Douglass' participations in separate colored workers organizations such as the American League of Colored Laborers in New York, 1850, and the Colored National Labor Union of which he was elected president in 1871.

Two questions asked by Douglass are relevant today. He opposed the great exodus of Negroes from the South in 1879, partly because "If it were conceded that the Federal government could not provide . . . protection [to person and property] in the South, what should be the final stopping-place for the Negro?" Even more trenchant and relevant was the question posed by Douglass in the *A.M.E. Review* in October 1889, when he asked whether "American justice, American liberty, American civilization, American law and American Christianity could be made to include and protect alike and forever all American citizens in the rights which have been guaranteed to them by the organic and fundamental laws of the land." His query was met by a resounding no. That negative response remains unchanged in 1971 while the Nixon administration seeks to win an unwinnable war, so we are told, that would deny to many of the people of South Vietnam, Cambodia, Laos, and perhaps Thailand the organic and fundamental laws which are also denied to Negro Americans, Indian Americans, Chicanos, Appalachian whites, and the poor regardless of their national origin or sex.

In personal appearance, Douglass and Du Bois were dissimilar. At the funeral of Douglass, a letter was read from Mrs. Elizabeth Cady Stanton, the great leader of the fight for abolition and for equal rights for women who had appeared on many a platform with Douglass. As she remembered him, "He stood there like an African prince, conscious of his dignity and power, grand in his proportions, majestic in his wrath, as with keen wit, satire and indignation he portrayed the bitterness of slavery." Portraits of him in his old age substantiate Mrs. Stanton's vivid recollection of him in the prime of his life.

When I first met Dr. Du Bois at the Gare St. Lazare, Paris, in the summer of 1921, and as photographs of the period confirm, he was rather slender. He looked not unlike the well-known photograph showing him leading an NAACP parade in 1917 which protested lynching and mob violence in the United States. He was no towering giant like Douglass; on the contrary, he was below medium height. I recognized him by what Miss Jessie Fauset, my former teacher of French at M Street High School, had called in her letter to me "his noble head." His dignity was hardly less than that described of Douglass by Mrs. Stanton. In his later years, Dr. Du Bois became somewhat corpulent and his head and face even more noble. I like to remember him as he looked in July 1958, the last time I saw him. The photograph of his head and upper torso by Scurlock Studio, taken probably in 1946, is one that should be in the library of all schools and colleges as well as private homes where great men are revered. He still wore his famous Prussian-like mustache and his equally famous Van Dyke beard. Most fascinating to me were his eyes, slightly sardonic, almost inscrutable as though he were looking behind the Veil of Color which he mentioned so often in his writings. Or perhaps better, he was trying to pierce the "plate glass" which even so careful scholars as Gunnar Myrdal and his associates called "glass plate" in *An American Dilemma* (pp. 680, 724-25). Since the "plate glass" is less well known than the Veil, I quote this passage from Du Bois' *Dusk of Dawn* (pp. 130-31):

It is difficult to let others see the full psychological meaning of caste segregation. It is as though one, looking out
from a dark cave in a side of an impending mountain, sees
the world passing and speaks to it; speaks courteously and
persuasively, showing them how these entombed souls are
hindered in their natural movement, expression, and development; and how their loosening from prison would
be a matter not simply of courtesy, sympathy and help to
them, but aid to all the world. One talks on evenly and
logically in this way, but notices that the passing throng
does not even turn its head, or if it does, glances curiously
and walks on. It gradually penetrates the minds of the
prisoners that the people passing do not hear; that some
thick sheet of invisible but horribly tangible plate glass is
between them and the world.

The relevance of this poetic prose, written in 1940, to 1971
needs no underscoring. Du Bois then described the despair
of the entombed souls and the continued indifference of
those on the other side of the plate glass. In a terrifying
sentence that could have been written in 1971, Du Bois
added: "They [the entombed souls] may even, here and
there, break through in blood and disfigurement, and find
themselves faced by a horrified, implacable, and quite overwhelming mob of people frightened for their own very
existence."

It is not improbable that some of the writing and proof-
ing of these pages of *Dusk of Dawn* was done in Baltimore.
In 1938, his daughter, Mrs. Yolande Du Bois Williams, was
living at 1532 McCulloch Street, and I have two prized
letters from Dr. Du Bois when he resided at 2302 Monte-
bello Terrace in August 1940. My puckish humor has led
me to place the inscribed copy of *Dusk of Dawn* next to an
inscribed copy of J. Edgar Hoover's book *J. Edgar Hoover
on Communism*. Published in 1969, this book asserted that

in 1964 the American Communist party "established the W. E. B. DuBois [sic] Clubs of America as a youth front." Listen carefully to the next sentence in the book: "This group, named after a famous Negro educator, author, and leader who joined the Communist party at the age of ninety-three, is the 'fingers of the party' on campuses." Remember the little-known praise given to Dr. Du Bois by Mr. Hoover when you read the allegation attributed to the latter that contributions to The Boys Clubs had greatly decreased because many persons thought they were Du Bois Clubs.

I suspect that in 1971 the Du Bois Clubs are better known than the Du Bois Circle of Baltimore, one of my principal reasons for saying earlier that Baltimore is an appropriate place to commemorate the life and works of this Bronze Titan. It was my privilege and honor to speak twice to the Du Bois Circle. On the invitation of Mrs. G. Clara Rhetta, acting chairman of the program committee, I addressed the club on December 19, 1939, at the home of Mrs. S. Elisabeth Fernandis, 1912 Druid Hill Avenue. Another of my cherished possessions is the Yearbook of the Du Bois Circle for 1939-1940. It lists the officers, members of the executive committee, the program committee, the speakers for the year, and thirty active members, two of whom lived in Washington. One of the five honorary members was Dr. W. E. B. Du Bois.

On the invitation of Mrs. Erma B. Davis, I had the honor of being the speaker on May 24, 1946, at the Madison Avenue YWCA, to commemorate the fortieth anniversary of the founding of the DuBois Circle. I salute the Du Bois Circle, which will soon celebrate its sixty-fifth anniversary, and venture to hope that the circle will facilitate the research which would result in a history of this organization. It was founded in the same year that Dr. Du Bois made what is still probably the most eloquent, succinct, and forth-right demand for equal rights for Negroes. At the second meeting of the Niagara Movement, Harpers Ferry, August 15, 1906, he warned: "We will not be satisfied to take one jot or tittle less than our full manhood rights. We claim for ourselves every single right that belongs to a freeborn American, political, civil and social; and until we get these rights we will never cease to protest and assail the ears of America."

Neither Douglass nor Du Bois were demigods or super-men. By trying to make the Colored National Labor Union an arm of the Republican party, Douglass hastened its demise. In 1872 he declared that the "Republican party is the ship, all else the sea." In his 1877 lecture, in Douglass Hall, Baltimore, a building named for him and used for educational purposes, he gave exaggerated praise to the nation's Capitol when he said: "Under its lofty domes and stately pillars, as under the broad blue sky, all races and colors of men stand upon a footing of common equality."

Du Bois swung almost full circle from his role of what I have called "an authentic American radical" at Harpers Ferry in 1906 to that of a fervent Communist in 1961. He gave up his American citizenship and became a citizen of Ghana. Meanwhile, he had abandoned his claim for "full manhood rights" and became in the early 1930s an advo-cate of "voluntary segregation." Less well known is his statement in 1944: "I did not believe that the Communism of Russia was the program for America; least of all for a minority group like the Negroes; I saw that the program of the American Communist party was suicidal." In his *Auto-biography,* edited by Herbert Aptheker, this sentence is changed to read: "I saw that the program of the American Communist party was inadequate for our plight." Even this change in Du Bois' language leaves unanswered the question about the reasons for his apostasy in 1961. (Dr. Aptheker has since written me that the sentence quoted in the *Autobiography* was that which appeared in the Du Bois papers.)

As an avowed disciple of the authentic American radicalism of Du Bois and a proponent of the thought, as I said on May 7, 1970, at Howard University, that "The Talented Tenth" will rise again, I am forced to conclude that inconsistency was the most evident characteristic of his life of almost a century. This inconsistency was well-nigh inevitable. He grew up during the restoration of white supremacy in the Southern states, its abject acceptance by the federal government, Northern magazines and newspapers, social gospelers, the secular clergy, business, and organized labor. He later witnessed the rise and fall of the Populist movement, Theodore Roosevelt's wooing simultaneously or by turns the "mutually hostile Black-and-Tans, Lily-whites and White-Supremacy Democrats," the specious progressivism of Woodrow Wilson, World War I, the "Red Summer" which followed it, the establishment of the Soviet Union, the ineffably stupid "return to normalcy" under Harding, the "Keep Cool with Cal," Hoover's bumbling which hastened the Great Depression, Franklin D. Roosevelt's inadequate New Deal, the waning of Truman's sturdy efforts to make civil rights meaningful for Negroes, Eisenhower's less than enthusiastic support of those rights, and Kennedy's support which was prompted at least in some measure by the brutal violence inflicted upon Freedom Riders and others engaged in nonviolent resistance. Meanwhile, his prophecy at the Pan-African Conference in London, 1900, that "the problem of the twentieth century is the problem of the color line" had been largely vindicated, but his four Pan-African congresses had produced few

tangible results. It was not until World War II had weak-
ened and impoverished the colonial powers that Winston
Churchill had to "preside over" the beginning of the liqui-
dation of the British Empire, de Gaulle had to concede
self-government and independence to most of France's
overseas non-self-governing and trust territories and departments, and Belgium to grant independence to the Belgian
Congo. When Du Bois died on August 27, 1963, practically
all of Africa down to "Southern Africa" was independent.
In Portuguese Africa, Rhodesia, the Republic of South
Africa, and Namibia (formerly Southwest Africa), the
"problem of the twentieth century" will still be, according
to the dire predictions of some observers, the problem of
the twenty-first century.

Even though Du Bois, after being briefly handcuffed
during his arraignment, was found in November 1951 inno-
cent of the accusation that he was the unregistered "agent
of a foreign principal," the Soviet Union, when Justice
McGuire gave a directed verdict of acquittal, yet today
some persons are afraid to honor him. Less well known
are the accusations that Douglass was a Negro first and an
American afterward because, when he was minister to
Haiti, Admiral Bancroft Gherardi, backed by some American businessmen and practically the entire United States
Navy, failed in 1891 to coerce Haiti into granting to the
United States a naval station at Môle Saint Nicolas. In his
*Life and Times*, Douglass disavowed any responsibility for
the failure to coerce Haiti into granting Môle Saint Nicolas
to the United States. But, because he refused to press upon
the president of Haiti what he considered a "plainly dishonest and scandalous" proposal made by the William P.
Clyde Company, he was characterized in the American
press as "more a Haitian than an American." "My own
belief," as I wrote in 1941 in *The Diplomatic Relations of*

*the United States with Haiti, 1776-1891,* "is that Douglass was sincerely desirous of protecting the interests of a country of the same race as his own but that he carried out his instructions as faithfully as would have any representative of the United States." That is still my belief.

At the time I wrote *The Diplomatic Relations,* I either did not know or had forgotten a now frequently quoted passage from Du Bois in *The Conservation of Races,* Occasional Paper No. 2 of the American Negro Academy, 1897. He asked: "What, after all, am I? Am I an American or am I Negro? Can I be both? Or is it my duty to cease to be a Negro as soon as possible and be an American? If I strive as a Negro, am I not perpetuating the very cleft that threatens Black and White America? Is not my only possible practical aim the subduction of all that is Negro in me to the American? Does my black blood place upon me any more obligation to assert my nationality than German, or Irish or Italian blood would?" I suspect that Douglass may have asked himself a similar question during the period that he was minister to Haiti.

In the *Atlantic Monthly,* 1897, and in *The Souls of Black Folk,* 1903, Du Bois described the dilemma in these eloquent words: "One ever feels his two-ness—an American, a Negro; two souls, two thoughts, two unreconciled strivings; two warring ideals in one dark body, whose dogged strength alone keeps it from being torn asunder. . . . He [the American Negro] simply wishes it possible for a man to be both a Negro and an American, without being spit upon by his fellows, without having the doors of opportunity closed roughly in his face."

This "two-ness," the conviction that he could not be both a Negro and an American, may well be one explanation for his joining the Communist party and renouncing his American citizenship. Like many other Negro Americans,

I confess to a "two-ness," but perhaps because I am only seventy-four and not ninety-three, for the time being at least I am going to remain a disciple of the Du Bois of 1906 and continue to strive here to help gain "our full manhood rights."

In February 1971, there are not many encouraging reasons for Negroes and many others to continue the struggle "within the system." One ray of hope lies in the belated honors conferred upon Du Bois. No white American college or university gave him an honorary degree. But Roy Wilkins had the courage to praise him at the Lincoln Memorial exercises climaxing the March on Washington for Jobs and Freedom on August 28, 1963. The first topic at the opening session of the Eighty-third Annual Meeting of the American Historical Association in New York City, December 28, 1968, was "W. E. B. Du Bois (1868-1968): In Observance of the One Hundredth Anniversary of his Birth." On October 18, 1969, after a long controversy because of his membership in the American Communist party, a five-acre tract laid out around a plot of ground that was once the site of the Du Bois family home in Great Barrington was dedicated. Later this year Hill and Wang, Inc. will publish my book *W. E. B. Du Bois—A Profile*.

I do not make predictions, but I venture to guess that in the future more posthumous honors will be conferred upon Du Bois, more courses, in addition to those offered at Morgan State College and at Howard University, will become the rule rather than the exception, and more books will be written about this Bronze Titan.

On August 27, 1963, John O. Killens, James Baldwin, and Sidney Poitier were talking in the lobby of the Willard Hotel in Washington when "someone walked over to our group and said, 'The old man died.'" As Killens narrated the incident in his introduction to the 1969 American edi-

tion of *An ABC of Color*: "Just that. And no one asked,'What
old man?' We all knew who the old man was, because he
was our old man. He belonged to every one of us. And we
belonged to him. To some of us he was our patron saint,
our teacher and our major prophet." This, I avow, is a
glorious valedictory.

# VII. Sambos and Rebels

## *The Character of the Southern Slave*

by John W. Blassingame

It is one of the ironies of American historiography that scholars have generally based their characterization of slaves more on literary stereotypes than on research. Sambo, combining in his character the behavior generally ascribed to Uncle Remus, Jim Crow, and Uncle Tom, was the most pervasive and long-lasting of the literary stereotypes of the slave in antebellum Southern novels, plays, and essays. Indolent, faithful, humorous, loyal, dishonest, superstitious, improvident, and musical, Sambo was inevitably a clown and congenitally docile. Characteristically a house servant, Sambo had so much love and affection for his master that he was almost filiopietistic; his loyalty was all-consuming and self-immolating. In the Southern novel, Sambo was the epitome of devotion; he often fought and died heroically while trying to save his master's life. Yet Sambo had no thought of freedom; that was an empty boon compared to serving his master. As improbable as it may seem, many white historians accept this stereotype as a true characterization of most slaves. Was Sambo real, or a figment of the white man's imagination? If he was not real, why was the slave described so often in such terms by antebellum Southern whites? While the problem is complex, we can give brief answers to these questions.

The slaves played a significant role in creating the Sambo stereotype because they frequently wore the mask of humility and submissiveness when interacting with whites. But it was the kind of mask about which Paul Laurence Dunbar wrote:

> We wear the mask that grins and lies,
> It hides our cheeks and shades our eyes,—
> This debt we pay to human guile;
> With torn and bleeding hearts we smile,
> And mouth with myriad subtleties.
> Why should the world be overwise,
> In counting all our tears and sighs?
> Nay, let them only see us, while
>     We wear the mask.

Most slaves carefully hid their true personality traits from whites while adopting "sham" characteristics when interacting with them.

According to Lucy Ann Delaney, slaves lived behind an "impenetrable mask . . . how much of joy, of sorrow, of misery and anguish have they hidden from their tormentors!" On innumerable occasions the slaves' public behavior contradicted their private attitudes. For instance, they frequently pretended to love their cruel masters. Lewis Clarke argued that this was "the hardest work that slaves have to do. When any stranger is present we have to love them very much . . . [but when masters were sick or dying] Then they all look glad, and go to the cabin with a merry heart." Austin Steward discovered the same practice among his fellow slaves when his mistress died: "The slaves were all deeply affected by the scene; some doubtless truly lamented the death of their mistress; others rejoiced that she was no more . . . One of them I remember went to the pump and wet his face, so as to appear to weep with the rest." Similarly, when Jacob Stroyer's cruel master died, the slaves shed false tears: "Of course the most of them were glad that he was dead," and some said, " 'Thank God, massa gone home to hell.' "

The slaves dissembled, they feigned ignorance and humility. If their masters expected them to be fools, they would play the fool's role. The slave frequently pretended to be much more humble than he actually was. When Jermain Loguen returned after an absence of several months to his rather despicable master, for example, he pretended to be happy. He wrote that he "went through the ceremony of servile bows and counterfeit smiles to his master and mistress and other false expressions of gladness." Later, Loguen fought with his master.

Along with the slave's play-acting, there were several other compelling factors which caused Southern writers to portray Blacks as Sambos. Few of them had any relation to the slave's actual behavior. Instead, the slave was stereotyped as Sambo because he allegedly belonged to an inferior race with immutable characteristics and to a subordinate caste. Then, too, facing the withering attack of the abolitionists, the Southern writer had to prove that slavery was not an unmitigated evil. The loyal contented slave was a *sine qua non* in Southern literary propaganda. Whether he existed in fact was irrelevant to the Southern writer. Without Sambo, it was impossible to prove the essential goodness of Southern society.

However pervasive Sambo was in Southern literature, this is no reason for historians to accept the portrait as representative of most slaves. This is especially true since there was another stereotyped figure—let us call him Nat, the rebel—who rivaled Sambo in the universality and continuity of his literary image. Revengeful, bloodthirsty, cunning, treacherous, and savage, Nat was the incorrigible runaway, the poisoner of white men, the ravager of white women,

who defied all the rules of plantation society. Subdued and
punished only when overcome by superior numbers or firepower, Nat retaliated when attacked by whites, killed overseers and planters, or burned plantation buildings when he
was abused. Nat's customary obedience often hid his true
feelings, self-concept, unquenchable thirst for freedom,
hatred of whites, discontent, and manhood, until he vio-
lently demonstrated these traits.

James McCune Smith described the slave symbolized
by Nat perfectly in 1855. Smith asserted:

> Blows and insults he bore, at the moment, without resent-
> ment; deep but suppressed emotion, rendered him insensi-
> ble to their sting; but it was afterward, when the memory
> of them went seething through his brain, breeding a fiery
> indignation at his injured self-hood, that the resolve came
> to resist, and the time fixed to resist, and the time fixed
> when to resist, and the plot laid, how to resist; and he al-
> ways kept his self-pledged word. In what he undertook, in
> this line, he looked fate in the face, and had a cool, keen
> look at the relation of means to ends.

Southern whites often thought of their slaves in the
same way as Smith. From an analysis of the constantly re-
curring rumors of insurrections, it is obvious that many
whites considered Black slaves dangerous, insubordinate,
bold, evil, restless, turbulent, vengeful, barbarous, and malicious. The white man's fear and anxiety over the slave
was so deep and pervasive that it was sometimes patho-
logical. A group of whispering slaves, mysterious fires, or
almost any suspicious event caused alarm, apprehension,
and a deepening sense of paranoia among whites. It is clear
that many whites did not believe the slaves were innately
docile. Too many governors received requests for arms and
troops from thousands of whites, the U.S. Army marched

and countermarched too often, too many panic-stricken whites spent their nights guarding their neighborhoods to believe that most Southern whites equated the Sambo stereotype with the dominant slave personality.

There is overwhelming evidence that the whites had good reason to be paranoid. The slave's undying love for freedom, his intractability, and his resistance to bondage can be documented easily. The resistance began in Africa. Often, kidnapped Africans tried to escape on the long march to the coast and committed suicide by drowning, or refusing food or medicine, rather than be enslaved. They often mutinied while being transported to the New World and killed their white captors. In spite of their chains and lack of arms, the Africans rebelled so frequently that a number of ship owners took out insurance to cover losses from mutinies. In their study of the slave trade, historians Mannix and Cowley uncovered "fairly detailed accounts of fifty-five mutinies on slavers from 1699 to 1845, not to mention passing references to more than a hundred others. The list of ships 'cut off' by the natives—often in revenge for the kidnapping of freemen—is almost as long. On the record it does not seem that Africans submitted tamely to being carried across the Atlantic like chained beasts."

Early records indicate that the Africans continued to resist even after they landed in the New World. Many eighteenth-century travel accounts, memoirs, and slave notices show that a number of the newly imported Africans almost literally ran away as soon as their feet touched American soil. Even when they did not run away, the Africans were often obstinate, sullen, and uncooperative laborers. An English traveler observed in 1746 that the African captive, "if he must be broke, either from Obstinacy, or, which I am more apt to suppose, from Greatness of Soul, will require . . . hard Discipline . . . you would really be surpriz'd at their Perseverance . . . they often die before they can be conquer'd."

American-born slaves had as much "Greatness of Soul" as their African ancestors. The yearning for freedom came with the first realization of the finality, of the fact of slavery. Lunsford Lane claimed that his first realization that he was a chattel, a thing for the use of others, caused him deep anxiety: "I saw no prospect that my condition would ever be changed. Yet I used to plan in my mind from day to day, and from night to night, how I might be free." In spite of all the floggings, there were hopes and dreams.

While it is impossible to measure exactly the extent of the slave's desire for freedom and dissatisfaction with his lot, it appears that the relationship between master and slave was one continual tug of war. According to the Louisiana slave Allen Parker, "There was always a kind of strife between master and slave, the master on the one hand trying to get all the work he possibly could out of the slaves . . . and the slaves . . . trying to get out of all the work they could, and to take every possible advantage of their master. . . ." As a result of this strife, most slaves grudgingly labored for their masters and tried to repress their anger.

Strong-willed blacks often repressed their anger, but they were not broken by the lash. William H. Heard declared that in spite of the cruel treatment meted out to the slaves, "many of them were never conquered." Rather than cower before the overseer's lash, the slaves often cursed the man who inflicted the pain on them. Frederick Douglass reported that one slave woman, after being flogged severely, "was not subdued, for she continued to denounce the overseer, and to call him every vile name. He had bruised her flesh, but had left her invincible spirit undaunted." On many occasions the slaves proved their indomitability by refusing to cry out under the lash. Elizabeth Keckley, for instance, initially resisted the effort of her master to flog her, and when he succeeded in doing so, she recalled that it was agonizing but did not break her spirit: "Oh, God! I can feel the torture now—the terrible, excruciating agony of those moments. I did not scream; I was too proud to let my tormentor know what I was suffering."

Many of the strongest, most industrious, and intelligent slaves refused to submit passively to floggings. William Wells Brown recalled that there was one strong and valuable slave on his plantation who had never been flogged and often declared "that no white man should ever whip him—that he would die first."

The relationship of the planters and overseers to the recalcitrant slave was a strange one. They feared the unruly slave, particularly if he was noted for his strength and vindictiveness. Inevitably, the unruly slave forced the master to be wary. There were certainly many masters who were cautious with slaves like Louis Manigault's Jack Savage, who was, he wrote, "the only Negro ever in our possession who I considered capable of murdering me or burning my dwelling at night or capable of committing any act." Then, there were slaves like the Black woman who told a group of Virginia whites that "If old mistress did not leave her alone and quit calling her a bitch and a strumpet, she would take an iron and split her brain. . . ." On innumerable occasions planters refused to punish such slaves unless they could get them drunk, surprise them, or get other slaves or whites to overpower them. In most cases the masters tried to avoid trouble with the intractable slave because of his value as a worker. Realizing this, many slaves parlayed it into better treatment: they threatened to run away, to fight, or to stop work if they were abused. For instance, William Green, after fighting his master to a standstill when the latter tried to flog him for disobedience, declared that no man would whip him and that if he were flogged, he would cease work. His master relented, Green declared, and "after this we made up and got along very well for almost a year." Similarly, James Mars asserted that he refused to permit his master to flog him when he was sixteen, and from that time until he was twenty-one he had no more trouble with his master: "I do not remember that he ever gave me an unpleasant word or look."

One of the most significant ways of resisting bondage was to run away. The slave who decided to follow the North Star to freedom, however, faced almost insurmountable obstacles. The most formidable obstacle he had to overcome was the psychological barrier of having to leave a home, friends, and family he loved. Mothers and wives argued passionately against it. Frederick Douglass felt that "thousands would escape from slavery . . . but for the strong cords of affection that bind them to their families, relatives and friends." Considering the likelihood of punishment and a harder life in case of failure, ridicule from the other slaves, the slave's ignorance of the world and of geography, his penniless condition, his viewing every white man as his enemy, and his memory of his master's tales of the horrible fate which befell fugitives who succeeded in reaching the North, a slave had to think a long time before he took the first step to permanent freedom. William Green and his friends often talked about escaping to Canada, but he declared that "it requires all the nerve and energy that a poor slave can bring to his support to enable him to make up his mind to leave in this precarious manner." On the eve of his escape from bondage, Frederick Douglass expressed what most slaves probably felt upon contemplating escape from slavery: "I was making a leap in the dark. . . . I was like one going to war without weapons—ten chances of defeat to one of victory."

One of the most objective and revealing sources of information on the character of the fugitives appears in the runaway slave notices in antebellum Southern newspapers. Unbiased attempts of owners to recover property worth hundreds of dollars, the notices were carefully composed, dispassionate descriptions of the fugitives, indicating their character, clothing, motives, and identifying marks. Most of the fugitives were young, robust men. In Louisiana most of them were between the ages of sixteen and twenty-five. Similarly, in a collection of 134 runaway slave notices from eighteenth-century newspapers, 76 per cent of the fugitives were under thirty-five and 89 per cent of them were men.

Most state studies of slavery indicate that there was no uniformity of personality types among the fugitives. For instance, Orville W. Taylor systematically examined notices in Arkansas newspapers and asserted that they showed "among other things, that slaves were as individualistic as white people, despite the regimentation of slavery." The major thing to remember about the slave notices is that they contained information which would help to distinguish the fugitive from the mass of slaves. It would appear from the notices that most fugitives had no readily identifiable behavioral patterns which set them apart from their fellows.

Those fugitives who were different in character from most slaves fell into two relatively broad categories. One group was composed of what Southerners called Sambo, the slave who allegedly viewed his master as his father and identified with his interest. The fugitive Sambo as described in the notices often stuttered, whined, laughed, grinned, trembled, was "easily frightened or scared," "rather stupid," "addicted to lying," or had a "sly," "down guilty" look, or "shiffled" and had a "low voice" or "a small impediment in speech when frightened" in the presence of whites.

The Sambo of the notices was a very complex fellow.

Frequently, in the same sentence in which the terms cited above appeared, the planters observed that the slave was artful, could read and write, and had probably forged a pass, and stolen money, horses, and clothes. A Virginia planter asserted in 1784 that the runaway Dick had "a very roguish down look ... is artful and plausible. ...."

The fugitive Sambo was a bundle of contradictions. On the one hand, he was the epitome of loyalty and docility, and completely trusted by his master. On the other, in spite of his sham "loyalty," he ran away. A South Carolina master in 1786 indicated how much of an enigma Sambo was when he observed that one of his fugitive slaves was

> sensible and artful, speaks quick, and sometimes stutters a little; HE MAY POSSIBLY HAVE A TICKET THAT I GAVE HIM TWO DAYS BEFORE HE WENT AWAY, DATED THE 6TH OF APRIL, MENTIONING HE WAS IN QUEST OF A RUNAWAY, AS I DID NOT MENTION WHEN HE WAS TO RETURN, HE MAY ENDEAVOR TO PASS BY THAT. ...

How could a slave so completely gain the confidence of his master that he would be sent out to look for a runaway slave and then become a fugitive himself?

Did Sambo grin and look down all the while that he was "artfully" and "ingeniously" planning to escape? Was he only play-acting when he grinned? Did he reveal his true character when he stepped out of the Sambo role or did the master misperceive his character, read too much into his "down look," while being selectively inattentive to his artfulness and roguish behavior?

The other character type which appears in the notices is the rebellious slave. The rebellious fugitive was very artful, cunning, a "well set, hardy villain," "of good sense, and much ingenuity," "saucy," "very surly," a "very great rogue," "sober and intelligent," "bold," "fights like the Devil when arrested," and often stole large sums of money and took along a "nice short shot gun." Many of these fugitives were habitual runaways and quick to try to get revenge when punished. The archetype of the rebellious fugitive was "Sarah" whom a Kentucky planter described in 1822 as

> the biggest devil that ever lived, having poisoned a stud horse and set a stable on fire, also burnt Gen. R. Williams stable and stock yard with seven horses and other property to value of $1500. She was handcuffed and got away at Ruddles Mills on her way down the river, which is the fifth time she escaped when about to be sent out of the country.

When slaves lived near swamps, impenetrable forests, or near frontier areas, they often banded together in mass efforts to escape from bondage. After a Spanish decree welcomed English slaves to Florida in 1733, often as many as twenty South Carolina slaves marched in a body to the colony, sometimes killing whites along the way. The most impressive of the South Carolina incidents began at Stono in September 1739, when a group of slaves sacked and burned the armory. Then they began marching toward a Spanish fort in Florida which contained a colony of runaway slaves and was manned by a Black militia company. Beating a drum as they marched, the slaves attacked all of the plantations along the way, and killed twenty or thirty whites before a militia company killed or captured most of them.

For the most part, the possibility of a large body of slaves marching undetected to a free state was remote. Realizing this, many runaways built "free" or maroon communities in the swamps and mountains in the South. The maroon communities represented one of the gravest threats

to the planters. In the first place, these communities under-
mined the master's authority and emboldened other slaves
to join them. For example, a group of North Carolina
planters complained in December 1830 that "their slaves
are become almost uncontrollable. They go and come when
and where they please, and if an attempt is made to stop
them they immediately fly to the woods and there continue
for months and years committing depredations on our Cattle hogs and Sheep . . . patrols are of no use on account of
the danger they subject themselves to. . . ." Second, and
perhaps more important, the maroons often engaged in
guerrilla-like activities, plundering and burning plantations, stealing stock, and attacking, robbing, and murdering
whites. If the maroons obtained enough arms or allied themselves with poor whites and Indians, they could terrorize
almost any isolated white community.

A maroon was a resourceful black man who, once having obtained his freedom, challenged any white man to take
it away from him. If his hide-out was discovered, he was
willing to die defending it. For instance, when a group of
North Carolina whites attacked a maroon camp in August
1856, the slaves fought back and killed one of them. Then,
the "negroes ran off cursing and swearing and telling them
to come on they were ready for them again."

The largest semipermanent maroon communities grew
up in areas where there was international rivalry over borders, or near sympathetic Indian tribes. In this regard, the
closest relations between red and Black men developed in
Florida when a branch of the Creek tribe, the Seminoles,
moved into the Spanish territory. Some of the Seminoles
owned Black slaves who were almost indistinguishable from
free men. These Blacks were joined by groups of runaway
slaves from South Carolina and Georgia who accepted the
Spanish invitation to desert their Protestant masters. By

1836 there were probably about twelve hundred maroons living in the Seminole towns. Better acquainted with whites than the Indians, the Black maroons and slaves often acted as interpreters for their red masters. By the mid-nineteenth century so many of the Indians and Blacks had intermarried that they were almost indistinguishable.

Aided by Indian wars and Spanish and British intrigues on the Georgia-Alabama border with Florida, large numbers of slaves escaped and joined the maroons. A special inducement was held out to runaways when during the War of 1812 the British built a fort on the eastern side of the Appalachicola River for themselves and their Black and red allies. Abandoning the fort in 1816 but leaving behind guns and cannon for their allies, the British inadvertently incited the First Seminole War. Three hundred runaway slaves immediately took over the fort. Led by the maroon Garcon, the runaways attacked a group of sailors from a U.S. gunboat in July and scalped most of them. After a short artillery duel the gunboat was successful in blowing up the fort's magazine, killing most of the Blacks. The survivors were recaptured and returned to their owners.

Seeking revenge for their fallen comrades, the Negroes and Indians began drilling in separate units under their officers. In 1817 and 1818 between 400 and 600 runaways joined with the Seminoles in raiding plantations in Georgia, killing the whites and liberating slaves. On April 16, 1818, Andrew Jackson captured one of the Seminole towns in which the Blacks, after their initial retreat, fought valiantly. Unable to follow the survivors into the trackless swamps, Jackson unilaterally ended what he called "this savage and negro war."

The presence of hundreds of runaway slaves plagued every effort to make a permanent peace with the Seminoles before 1865. The immediate cause of the Second Seminole War was intimately related to the problem of the maroons. The war can be traced to the kidnapping and the return to slavery of a daughter of a Negro fugitive who was the wife of the Seminole chief, Osceola. As a result of this, in December 1835 the Indians, after being informed of the route of a company of American soldiers by a Negro guide, massacred about one hundred of the troops. Negro warriors fought in most of the battles during the next seven years and were so numerous in some of them that on one occasion General Thomas Jesup declared: "This, you may be assured, is a negro, not an Indian war. . . ."

The character of the Black maroons emerges clearly from the official records. In a typical report, an army officer asserted that "The Negroes, from the commencement of the Florida war, have, for their numbers, been the most formidable foe, more blood-thirsty, active and revengeful than the Indian. . . . Ten resolute negroes, with a knowledge of the country, are sufficient to desolate the frontier, from one extent to the other." The war ended in 1842 only after Zachary Taylor guaranteed the Black maroons that they would be removed to the Southwest.

In spite of widespread maroon activity and individual resistance among slaves in the South, there have been considerably fewer large-scale slave rebellions in the United States than in Latin America. The explanation for this lies in the differences between conditions in Latin America and in the South. A chronic shortage of military forces and a high slave to white population ratio (7 to 1 in the British West Indies, 11 to 1 in Haiti, 20 to 1 in Surinam) severely limited the ability of Latin Americans to control plantation Blacks. Faced with an underdeveloped communication and transportation network, along with the propinquity of plantations to jungles, swamps, and mountains, Latin American masters found it difficult to prevent slaves from rebelling or escaping to the "trackless wilderness." When the slaves did escape to the almost impenetrable forest, they were able to form free communities in relative security. The military forces were so weak that it once took a Cuban army two months to dislodge 700 slaves from a mountain stronghold, while a colonial Mexican army took months to reach the site of a slave rebellion in the mining region and then could not defeat the rebels. Although an ignorant slave may not have known in advance that the army was weak, the existence of the slave communities was public knowledge. The communities stood, moreover, as an open invitation for the slave to escape and a monument to the weakness of the master class. Besides, he had before him the knowledge and tradition of successful slave resistance. Of overriding importance in the apparent greater inclination of Latin American slaves to rebel was the constant importation of Africans and a slave population composed of from 60 to 70 per cent males.

Having the advantage over their Latin American counterparts in practically every respect, Southern planters were able to crush every slave rebellion with relative ease, and more importantly, to prevent the development of a tradition of successful revolt in the quarters. Unless he was totally blind, a slave could not fail to perceive how hopeless revolt was, given the size and undeniably superior firepower of the whites. In this regard, the few revolts which did occur in the United States are convincing evidence of the indomitability of the slave. After all, he had far less chance of success than his Latin American brother.

There has been so much controversy surrounding the whole question of slave rebellions that one has to apply a very strict definition to the word "revolt." A revolt is defined in this study as any concerted effort by a group of slaves to destroy the lives and property of local whites which led public officials to call out the militia. Applying this rigid definition, there were nine slave revolts in America between 1691 and 1865. Although most of the large-scale conspiracies occurred in cities, most of the actual rebellions took place in plantation counties.

A few of these revolts must be analyzed in order to understand the full range of the Black man's reaction to slavery. In 1712 several Africans formed a plot in New York City to burn the town, destroy all whites "for some hard usage they apprehended to have received from their masters," and to obtain their freedom. Sealing an oath of secrecy by sucking each other's blood and rubbing powder prepared by a Black conjurer on their bodies to make them invincible, the conspirators armed themselves with guns, pistols, swords, daggers, knives, and hatchets. On the night of April 6, they set fire to several buildings and then murdered and wounded at least sixteen whites who came to put out the blaze. When the alarm was sounded and troops called out, the rebels retreated. They were later captured and convicted. Some were either burned alive, hung, or broken on the wheel.

A larger uprising occurred in Louisiana's St. Charles and St. John the Baptist parishes in 1811. Led by a free Negro, Charles Deslondes, 400 slaves killed 2 whites and burned several plantations in St. John early in January. Gaining adherents along the Mississippi River, the insurgents formed into units of as many as 500 slaves and began marching the thirty-one miles to New Orleans. Before they reached the city, U.S. troops attacked and killed 66 slaves in open battle. Later, 16 leaders were executed in New Orleans and their heads were placed on poles on roads leading from the city.

The most destructive of all the slave revolts occurred

near Jerusalem, Southampton County, Virginia, in 1831. Fortunately, a white lawyer, Thomas R. Gray, recorded the confession of "the leader of this ferocious band" and "the origin and progress of this dreadful conspiracy." According to Gray, the rebellion "was not instigated by motives of revenge or sudden anger, but the results of long deliberation and a settled purpose of mind." Nat Turner, the arch-rebel, was a precocious child who was strongly influenced by his parents and especially his father, who had escaped from slavery. After a series of mystical experiences and visions, Nat and his co-conspirators led a rebellion which left a bloody trail of battered heads across Southampton before they were captured.

A short, coal-black man, Turner was fearless, honest, temperate, religious, and extremely intelligent. Gray asserted that Turner, "for natural intelligence and quickness of apprehension, is surpassed by few men I have ever seen." He knew a great deal about military tactics, and had a "mind capable of attaining anything. . . ." Feeling no remorse for the fifty-five whites killed during the rebellion, Turner calmly contemplated his execution. Gray gave the best characterization of him when he wrote:

> He is a complete fanatic, or plays his part most admirably.
> . . . The calm, deliberate composure with which he spoke
> of his late deeds and intentions, the expression of his fiend-
> like face when excited by enthusiasm, still bearing the
> stains of blood of helpless innocence about him; clothed
> with rags and covered with chains; yet daring to raise his
> manacled hands to heaven, with a spirit soaring above the
> attributes of man; I look on him and my blood curdled in
> my veins.

The Black slaves "curdled" the blood of many Southern whites. The ubiquitous runaway was the "bogey man" for young whites, "troublesome property" for his master, and a hero in the quarters. In light of the record of slave resistance, it is a criminal libel against history for such men as Stanley Elkins to assert that most slaves were Sambos. Instead of the childlike and submissive Sambo being the dominant slave personality, there was great diversity in slave character. A former Missouri slave, Henry Clay Bruce, gave the most accurate portrayal of the captive Blacks and the best summary for this lecture long ago:

> There were different kinds of slaves, the lazy fellow, who would not work at all unless forced to do so, and required to be watched, the good man, who patiently submitted to everything. . . . Then there was the unruly slave, whom no master particularly wanted for several reasons: first, he would not submit to any kind of corporal punishment; second, it was hard to determine which was the master or which the slave; third, he worked when he pleased to do so. . . . This class of slaves were usually industrious, but very impudent. There were thousands of that class, who spent their lives in their master's service doing his work undisturbed, because the master understood the slave . . . there were thousands of high-toned and high spirited slaves, who had as much self-respect as their masters. . . . These slaves knew their own helpless condition. . . . But . . . they did not give up in abject servility. . . .

# VIII. Black History's Diversified Clientele

by Benjamin A. Quarles

Along with many other denials since he arrived on these shores, the Black American has until recently been denied a past. The consequent damage to his psyche can hardly be imagined. In a poem entitled "Negro History," appearing in the volume *From the Ashes: Voices of Watts* (Budd Schulberg, editor), young Jimmie Sherman depicts the past as his grandfather viewed it:

> A ship
> A chain
> A distant land
> A whip
> A pain
> A white man's hand
> A sack
> A field
> of cotton balls—
> The only things
> Grandpa recalls.

Such an outlook on the past has a stultifying effect, making for apathy and despair. Hence, Black leaders since the birth of the Republic have been advocates of Negro history, obviously envisioning a far broader coverage of it than Jimmie Sherman's grandpa had come to know. Black scholars, led by Carter G. Woodson in 1915, began to remove the layers of ignorance and distortion that had encrusted the Afro-American past. One of these scholars, W. E. B. Du Bois, in the closing line of his autobiography, written during his last months, bespoke anew his lifelong devotion to history: "Teach us, Forever Dead, there is no Dream but Deed, there is no Deed but Memory." A quarter of a century earlier Du Bois fired back a sharp rejoinder to a magazine editor who had rejected a Du Bois essay because it had touched upon the past. "Don't you understand," Du Bois wrote, "that the past is present; that without what was, nothing is."

During the past decade the cry for Black history has been stronger than ever before. Numbered among the proponents of such history are the newer Black militants. "We Blacks," writes Imamu Amiri Baraka (LeRoi Jones), must "learn our collective past in order to design a collective destiny." Of his period of confinement at the Norfolk (Massachusetts) Prison Colony, Malcolm X wrote: "I began first telling my Black brother inmates about the glorious history of the Black man—things they had never dreamed." On another occasion he referred to history as "a people's memory" without which "man is demoted to the lower animals." In his assessment of the past, Malcolm X did not ignore the less glorious aspects of the Black pilgrimage in America. Speaking to a ghetto audience in Detroit in 1953 he evoked a deep response with the words: "We didn't land on Plymouth Rock, my brothers and sisters —Plymouth Rock landed on *us!*"

Eldridge Cleaver, who, like Malcolm X, became a serious student of history while serving time in prison, spoke its praises. In his essay "To All Black Women, From All Black Men," in *Soul on Ice,* he writes:

> Be convinced, Sable Sister, that the past is no forbidden
> vista upon which we dare not look, out of a phantom fear
> of being, as the wife of Lot, turned into pillars of salt.
> Rather the past is an omniscient mirror: we gaze and see
> reflected there ourselves and each other—what we used to
> be and what we are today, how we got this way, and what
> we are becoming. To decline to look into the Mirror of
> Then, my heart, is to refuse to view the face of Now.

One of the sable sisters who has needed no convincing
about history's role is poet Sarah Webster Fabio, who
writes:

> Now at all costs, we must heal our history.
> Or else our future rots in the disease of
> our past.

Although Black history is now coming into its own as
never before, not all of its proponents are in pursuit of the
same goal. Indeed, today Black history is being called upon
to serve an increasing variety of publics, four of whom we
may scrutinize briefly. These are the Black rank and file,
the Black revolutionary nationalists, the Black academicians, and the white world, both scholarly and lay. Not
mutually exclusive, these groups often overlap. But this
fourfold typology enables us to illustrate the major contemporary uses of Black history. We may take these in
turn, first describing their aims and then noting their general content and style.

For the Black rank and file, the man in the street, the
laity, Black history's main objective is to create a sense of
racial pride and personal worth. To the rank and file the
new Black history is good therapy, its end result an im-
proved self-image. In a world that has traditionally equated
blackness with inferiority, Black history serves as a balm

to make the wounded whole. In a world that has traditionally equated blackness with low aim, Black history serves as a stimulus to success. To a Black person seeking to resolve an identity crisis, Black history is ego-soothing; it places one in the thick of things, thereby diminishing his sense of alienation, of rootlessness. Black history is a search for the values and the strengths imbedded in the Black subculture. Black history strikes at the Black American's legacy of self-rejection, the burden of shame that he had been taught was his to bear going back to the curse of Cain. "I always wanted to be somebody," runs the title of the autobiography of a Black tennis champion. Black history tells the Black reader that he is somebody, however vicariously.

In its content, Black history for the masses reflects somewhat "the great man" theory of history. White or Black, the typical American, himself individualistic, conceives of his country's past as the achievements of a group of outstanding characters, pushing on against herculean odds. History is a tableau of heroes set in bold relief. To the generality of Blacks their men of mark constitute their history, the bulk of their attention falling upon individual achievers—an underground railroad conductor like Harriet Tubman, a dedicated bishop like Daniel E. Payne, an educator like Mary McLeod Bethune, a sports celebrity like prize fighter Peter Jackson or jockey Isaac Murphy, and a singer like Elizabeth Taylor Greenfield (the "Black Swan") or Bessie Smith. The list is endless, ranging from an early African king to a present-day ghetto leader.

Upbeat and achievement-oriented, Black history for the rank and file stresses victories—the peak that was scaled, the foe that was vanquished, the deep river that was crossed. Moreover, to the masses, youth makes a special appeal, the younger Frederick Douglass arousing more interest than the Sage of Anacostia. Local Black historical figures likewise meet with a readier response than out-of-staters, however more nationally important the latter may be. Moreover, history designed for the laity will of necessity devote as much attention to popular culture and the lively arts as to the more traditional staples, politics and economics, particularly since the Black stamp on the former is more readily discernible.

The emphasis on the lively arts and popular culture lends itself to the mass media. Hence, Black history for laymen has found a natural ally in television, commercial as well as educational, but obviously of far greater proportions in the latter. Radio, too, especially in the folkways recordings, lends itself to Black cultural history. Other mass media such as newspapers and magazines are increasingly carrying Black history articles, biographical sketches, and pictorial materials. Sensing the growing interest in Black history, commercial firms have brought out coloring books, alphabet books, Black history games, and Black history in comic-book format.

History as hero worship is hardly the kind of history espoused by the second Black group under survey—the Black revolutionary nationalists. This group focuses upon exploiters and oppressors, a case study in man's inhumanity to man. This group views history as grievance collecting, a looking back in anger. Black nationalist history is essentially the story of a powerful white majority imposing its will upon a defenseless Black minority. Black nationalists hold that American society needs to be reconstructed and that Black history is, or should be, a means of ideological indoctrination in the revolutionary cause of Black liberation.

Black nationalist history is not without its traces of paranoid thinking, one which holds that the forces of evil are banded in an eternal conspiracy to maintain their oppressive sway. Of very ancient origin, this devil theory of history is deeply rooted in the human psyche and hence should occasion no surprise when met in any of its multiple guises.

Like so much else in American life, Black nationalism has, as it has always had, a variety of forms—cultural, religious, and economic, among others. Revolutionary nationalism moves a step beyond the others in its goals and does not rule out violence in achieving them. Revolutionary Black nationalists, having carefully examined the almost unbelievable pervasiveness of color prejudice in our society have, in essence, given up on America. Estranged from the land of their birth, they ponder its dismantlement.

As to content, revolutionary Black history is not as interested in historical spadework as in providing new interpretations of that which is already known. Black nationalist history emphasizes racial contrast, physical and cultural. It propounds a Black aesthetic and implies a Black mystique. It bespeaks the essential kinship of Black people on whatever continent they be located or in whatever walk of life. Its central theme is oppression, slavery in one guise or another. Rebelliousness against the oppressor likewise looms large in nationalist lore.

A compound of Black rage and white guilt, revolutionary Black history makes much of the analogy of colonialism, holding that Black Americans live in a state of vassalage to white Americans. Black America is a semicolony of white America.

Going further, the revolutionary school of thought stresses separatism, insisting that Black Americans have always constituted a nation. To those who hold these views, Black history has one overriding purpose; namely, to promote nation-building.

In tone, Black revolutionary history is judgmental,

with overtones of recrimination, moral condemnation, and prophetic warning. Apocalyptic and polemical in temper, it scorns objectivity, which it equates with a defense of the status quo. Revolutionary Black history may, on occasion, read like social commentary, sometimes taking on a man-the-barricades urgency.

Selective in content, Black revolutionary history ignores as irrelevant those aspects of the past which do not relate to its philosophy. As will be noted in just a moment, however, this tendency to pick and choose is nothing new in the historical profession.

The third group under survey are the Black academicians—the intellectually sophisticated, the college and university trained, the well-read. Like the revolutionary nationalists, they operate on a more studious level. They would concur with the revolutionary nationalists in holding that history is a weapon in the warfare. But to the academically oriented mind the basic foe is ignorance, be it willful or otherwise. It hardly need be added that ignorance is a somewhat impersonal foe and hence less easily pinpointed, less starkly isolated.

To the Black academician, history is a discipline, an attempt to recapture and mirror the past as accurately as possible. Admittedly this is a tall order, considering the nature of the evidence and the unreliability of so many of the witnesses. Black academicians hardly need to be reminded that history, as we know it, is not neutral, not value-free. Who can tell the Black academician anything new about the insensitivity of past generations of white scholars, of their neglect or distortion of the role of Black peoples? But the Black academician would question the viewpoint that prejudiced history must be met with prejudiced history; he would doubt that the best way to strike at the mythmakers of history is to imitate them. In *The Fire Next*

*Time,* James Baldwin has observed that "an invented past can never be used; it cracks and crumbles under the pressures of life like clay in a season of drought." As we have noted, however, white Americans have made some use of an invented past. But Black Americans must realize that a powerful majority may for a time be able to afford the luxury of fantasy. Such indulgence on the part of a minority is a species of living beyond its means, a minority having to husband carefully its limited resources.

Like the layman and the nationalist, the Black academician finds in Black history a deepening sense of racial worth and of peoplehood. He, too, reads Black history with pride. The Black academician views America as a civilization upon which his ancestors have left their stamp. Hence, he does not regard America as a white civilization exclusively; to him it also has its Black, red, and yellow components. The Black academician holds that his forebears helped to build America, and this being the case no one should sensibly expect him to pack his belongings and leave for other shores.

In addition to personal and racial gratification, the Black academician reads Black history because he feels that it will contribute to his knowledge and understanding of mankind, of his fellow travelers in time and space.

For academicians, the content of Black history would be more selective than for the laymen, in an attempt to avoid the obvious or the well known. Black history for the academician would deal less with persons and more with processes, less with general Black history than with selected topics in Black history. It would include comparative studies and pose methodological problems. On the grounds that academicians do not shy away from the unpleasant, Black history for them would not ignore the less glorious aspects of the Black past—the African tribesmen who engaged in the slave trade, the slave drivers on the Southern plantations, the Black informers who divulged the slave conspiracies or those who revealed the hiding place of a runaway slave. History has its share of those Blacks who turned out to be all too human.

The academician would grant that, more often than not, the truth makes one sick. But he believes the New Testament adage about truth also making one free. The academician holds that truth, including the search for it, has a liberating effect. To be truly free is to be free first and foremost in the great franchise of the mind. To a group like Black Americans, who have been subjected to so much falsehood by others, it would seem that the quest for truth should be held in high favor, having a relevance never failing.

Black history written for the academic fraternity will in the main take on a reflective, judicial tone, taking its cue from the careful winnowing and sifting that preceded it. The style will be sober, the rhetoric restrained. Passionate and deeply emotional language is highly necessary and desirable in human affairs, but such expression is more the province of the poet, the orator, and the charismatic leader than of the professional historian. An orator may give full vent to his innnermost feelings, and to the innermost feelings of his audience, but a social scientist works in a discipline which has imperatives of its own, imperatives which may point to conclusions that run counter to his private wishes.

The codes of his discipline bring the Black academician face to face with one of the major problems confronting every social scientist; namely, whether his citizen role should overshadow his professional role, whether he should give priority to social action or to scientific inquiry. Should an academician strive for competence in his discipline or should he seek primarily to become personally involved and relevant? To the Black academician this dilemma takes on an unusual urgency inasmuch as he is fully aware of the long-standing discriminations against Black people in the American social order. Addressing himself to this question of citizenship role versus professional role, sociologist Ernest Q. Campbell comes to the conclusion that "there is no intrinsic reason why the roles of scientific inquirer and staunch advocate are incompatible" ("Negroes, Education, and the Southern States," *Social Forces*, March 1969). But to play these two roles simultaneously would seem to require unusual abilities and energies. In their absence each Black academician must come to some hard choices as to his own major commitment.

To the final audience under survey, the white community—academic and lay—Black history has an important message. Black history should not be confined to Blacks alone—this would be like confining the Gospel to those already converted, to use a familiar figure. Black history, like other phases of Black studies, is no longer a matter of limited concern. Whites need to know Black history. As Theodore Draper points out in *The Rediscovery of Black Nationalism* (New York, 1970), "In the interest of the entire society, white students need Black Studies as much or even more than black students." At a meeting of the Organization of American Historians in 1969, C. Vann Woodward voiced much the same sentiment in his presidential address, "Clio with Soul." Woodward spoke of Black history as being "too important to be left entirely to Negro historians."

To begin with, whites should realize that the major reason for the long neglect of Black history falls upon the historical guild itself. As Carl Becker has pointed out, "The historian selects from a number of particular facts certain

facts which he considers most important to be known."
Historians, continues Becker, "unconsciously read the objective facts of the past in the light of their own purposes,
or the preoccupations of their own age." To point out that
written history has a subjective element is certainly nothing
new—Becker's observations were made in 1910. But to mention this matter at the outset makes for the open-minded-
ness so essential to a proper perspective on the Black American. Whites who read history should know by now that
white historians have until recently dealt with the American past in such a way as to ignore the Black presence or
to minimize its importance in the making of America.

The aim of Black history for white readers is twofold;
first to eliminate the myth that our country's past was rosy
and romantic, a new Eden "with liberty and justice for all,"
and second, to illustrate the centrality of the Black American in our national experience. White historians have until
recently tended to play down the somber aspects of Black-
white relationships in America—the deeply ingrained sense
of white superiority dating back to Jamestown and Plymouth, the brutality of slavery, the mockery of post-Recon-
struction, and the twentieth-century offshoots of these
persistent pathologies. The American past has a tragic component which cannot be brushed away. White Americans
must need take a second thought as they sing the familiar
lines, "Thine alabaster cities gleam,/Undimmed by human
tears."

Black history would enable whites to more realistically
appraise some of our country's boasted achievements and
some of its acclaimed public figures. For example, whites
generally view the age of Andrew Jackson as one in which
the right to vote was extended to the common man. But
whites need to know that it was during this period that
states like North Carolina and Pennsylvania were explicitly

prohibiting Blacks from exercising this privilege. White readers of American history have thought highly of Woodrow Wilson for his espousal of the "New Freedom" and for his doctrine of "making the world safe for democracy." But white readers need to know that during Wilson's presidency, and with his acquiescence, Black federal workers in the District of Columbia were systematically segregated and were given inferior working conditions and restroom facilities such as had not existed up to this time in the federal government.

Black history would be remiss if it did not call attention to these sobering aspects of the American past. But Black history does not consist solely of white denial and discrimination. Hence Black history for whites would indicate the myriad ways in which this country's history and culture would have been different without the presence of the Black man. Many of these ways—economic, political, constitutional, and military—are more quickly spotted than others. In some fields—art, literature, music, the dance, and popular culture in general—the Black contribution centers in the common core, making its stamp more difficult to isolate. But whether obvious or subtle, the Black man's gifts to America have been freely received if slowly acknowledged. To this extent all Americans are part Black in their cultural patrimony. Blacks in general would concur in the sentiment expressed by a stanza fom James Weldon Johnson ("Fifty Years, 1863-1913," in his *Fifty Years and Other Poems,* Boston, 1921):

> This land is ours by right of birth,
> This land is ours by right of toil;
> We helped to turn its virgin earth,
> Our sweat is in its fruitful soil.

The acceptance of Black history by whites has been

greatly facilitated by the current emphasis on social history. "It is a good moment to be a social historian" writes E. J. Hobsbawn (*Daedalus*, Winter 1971), history professor at the University of London. This branch of history pays particular attention to the anonymous common man and to the manners and customs of everyday life. And even more importantly for a Black orientation, this branch of history emphasizes social movements and the phenomena of social protest.

For the white reader of Black history the content would, at least initially, suggest the centrality of the Negro American and his identification with this country's great, professed goals. Therefore such history would comprise a general presentation of the American past with the Black component interwoven throughout, appearing at its proper chronological juncture and not separately, somewhat like a disjointed subtheme for the curious, Clio's underworld.

In style and technique Black history for whites would differentiate between the white layman and the white intellectual. For the white layman the approach would be much the same as for his Black counterpart, that is, an emphasis on biographical sketches and on the lively arts and popular culture, including sports. Again, as for the Black layman, books would be greatly supplemented by the mass media. Indeed, of course, the mass media outlets used to reach Black people will inevitably reach many whites.

For the white academician the approach to Black history might be broader than the biographical and less fearful of the recipient's short attention span. Black studies for white intellectuals would back assertion with documentation, presenting proof and citing authorities. A footnote is not an end unto itself. But those of an academic bent have been trained to look for the hard evidence; to them a statement must be intellectually tenable, its sources as trustworthy as possible. For the open-minded scholar—the seeker after truth—the will to believe is not an acceptable substitute for the data that corroborates.

We have dealt with Black history for four different audiences. But in written history the use of different approaches and viewpoints need come as no surprise. No one category of events, no single interpretation, can furnish the cloth for that seamless garment we call history. There is no single compass by which to unravel the course of historical causation. Written history, in form and content, is many-sided, however much this may disconcert the doctrinaire types.

This short excursion into Black history has taken note of varying viewpoints as to its function. Although varied, these approaches are often complementary rather than contradictory. More than anything else they demonstrate that there are alternate ways of looking at the past. The viewpoints of the revolutionary nationalist and the academic historian are not necessarily antagonistic. The academician, for example, may disavow an activist role and say that he is dealing with ideas for their own sake. But ideas are weapons and, as a rule, action is germinated by ideas.

In the formation of the new Black history the academician—the traditionalist—will continue to be of major importance. But if Black history is to come of age, revolutionary Black nationalists will also have much to contribute. The nationalist historians will force a reexamination of the historic patterns of color prejudice in America, not only in its grosser, more obvious manifestations, but in its manifold subtle forms, its protective coloration, one might say. The nationalists will bring into purview the Blacks of the so-called Third World, comparing and contrasting them with their counterparts in America. The tone of moral outrage that characterizes the nationalist school has its value, too, a healthy anger often acting as a social catalyst.

And finally the revolutionary Black nationalist has made it clear that to properly assess the Black past we need newer, nontraditional techniques. A multidisciplinary approach is called for, one not relying so largely on written records. Historical inquiry is already profiting from the methodology of the behavioral sciences—sociology, anthropology, and psychology. Interdisciplinary history opens vistas across and beyond the traditional chronological and geographic boundaries. These widening approaches to appraising the past have led to such newer periodicals as the *Journal of Interdisciplinary History*, its first issue appearing in the autumn of 1970 and its avowed purpose to "stimulate historians to examine their own subjects in a new light, whether they be derived from psychology, physics, or paleontology."

This is the age of ideological cross-fertilization. It is to be noted, for example, that today in the study of early man on this planet no fewer than twelve different special skills are necessary—six field skills and six laboratory skills. In properly assessing the Black role in American history a comparable if less numerous list of skills is needed. Without the use of these newer tools the past will remain an incompleted past. In fine, historians of the Black past must take into consideration "the changing character of historical evidence, the development of new techniques and concepts in related disciplines, and the growing body of research by non-historians into historical problems," to borrow a phrase from David S. Landes and Charles Tilly ("History as Social Science," in Social Science Research Council *Items*, March 1971).

The newer Black history, looking afresh down the cor-

ridors of time, has a revolutionary potential of its own. For
Blacks it is a new way to see themselves. For whites it fur-
nishes a new version of American history, one that especially challenges our national sense of smugness and self-
righteousness and our avowal of fair play. Beyond this the
new Black history summons the entire historical guild—
writers, teachers, and learners—to higher levels of expec-
tation and performance. History, as all of its disciples know,
is both continuity and change. Change stems from our
readiness to challenge the current order, using the best
tools of our trade. A new Black history would revitalize
education, quickening whatever it touches.

In 1925 in the foreword to his pathbreaking volume
*The New Negro,* Alain Locke, one of the many illustrious
Howard University scholar-humanists, said many things
that have a contemporary ring: "Negro life is not only establishing new contacts and founding new centers, it is
finding a new soul. There is a fresh spiritual and cultural
focusing. . . . There is a renewed race-spirit that consciously
and proudly sets itself apart." Locke, of course, was speaking primarily of creative expression in the arts, but his
words aptly characterize the current Black thrust in history. In its work of restoring history's lost boundaries, the
Black history of today is establishing new contacts and finding a new soul.

# The Contributors

## WILLIAM LEO HANSBERRY

William Leo Hansberry was a pioneer in the study of African history and celebrated the history of the Black man with dignity, diligence, and devotion. He received the Bachelor of Arts degree in 1921 and the Master of Arts degree in 1932, both from Harvard University.

For over fifty years Hansberry collected various kinds of data on African history and accumulated an impressive personal collection of notes, lectures, speeches, and books pertaining to the whole field of African studies. A collection of these papers is located in the Moorland-Spingarn Research Center at Howard University. Professor Hansberry was a member of the faculty of Howard University from 1922 to 1959. The University of Nigeria awarded him the doctorate of letters in 1961 and established the Hansberry Institute of African Studies.

In September 1963 he became Distinguished Visiting Professor at the University of Nigeria. The first volume of a collection of Mr. Hansberry's essays, *Pillars in Ethiopian History: The William Leo Hansberry African History Notebook*, was recently published by the Howard University Press.

## CLIFTON F. BROWN

Clifton F. Brown is the director of the undergraduate program of the department of history, Howard University. He received the Bachelor of Arts degree from Central State University in 1965; the Masters of Arts degree in 1968, and the Masters of Religion degree in 1972, both from Howard University.

Mr. Brown is the co-author of the book *Afro-American Religious Studies,* published by Scarecrow Press in 1971. He has written several articles on European and African history.

## JOHN HOPE FRANKLIN

John Hope Franklin is a distinguished American historian of international reputation. He was graduated from Fisk University in 1935 with a Bachelor of Arts degree and received from Harvard University his Master of Arts degree in 1936 and his Doctor of Philosophy degree in 1941. Dr. Franklin has taught American history at Fisk University, St. Augustine's College, North Carolina College, Howard University, Brooklyn College, and the University of Chicago, where he was chairman of the department for three years and is now John Matthews Manly Distinguished Service Professor of History. He has been a Visiting Professor at Harvard University, the University of California (Berkeley), and the Salzburg Seminar. In 1960 Dr. Franklin was a Fulbright Professor in Australia, and from 1962 to 1963 a Pitt Professor of American History and Institutions at Cambridge University.

In recognition of his scholarship, Professor Franklin has been awarded honorary degrees by Morgan State College (LL.D., 1960), Virginia State College (LL.D., 1961), Lincoln University (LL.D., 1961), Cambridge University (A.M., 1962), Tuskegee Institute (LL.D., 1964), the University of Massachusetts (L.H.D., 1964), Lincoln College (LL.D., 1965), Hamline University (LL.D., 1965), Fisk University (LL.D., 1965), Howard University (LL.D., 1968), and other universities. Dr. Franklin is a member of Phi Alpha Theta, Phi Beta Kappa, and a Fellow of the American Academy of Arts and Sciences. In recent years he has served on the Council of the American Historical Association, and was reelected in December 1969. Currently he is president of the Southern Historical Association.

Professor Franklin's works include *The Free Negro in North Carolina* (1943); *From Slavery to Freedom: A History of Negro Americans* (1947; third edition, 1967); *The Militant South 1800-1861* (1956); *Reconstruction After the Civil War* (1961); *The Emancipation Proclamation* (1963); and with the editors of Time-Life an *Illustrated History of Black Americans* (1970). He has edited the *Civil War Diary of James T. Ayers* (1947); Albion Tourgee's *A Fool's Errand* (1961); Thomas Wentworth Higginson's *Army Life in a Black Regiment* (1962); and *Color and Race* (1968).

# OTEY M. SCRUGGS

Otey M. Scruggs was born in Vallejo, California, where he received his education in the public schools. In 1951 he earned the Bachelor of Arts degree from the University of California, Santa Barbara. He received the Doctor of Philosophy degree in 1958 from Harvard University.

Before assuming his present position as professor of history at Syracuse University, Dr. Scruggs taught United States history for a number of years at the University of California, Santa Barbara. In addition to teaching Afro-American history, he directs the graduate program in Afro-American history.

Professor Scruggs has published extensively in the area of the United States American labor movement. In 1963 he co-edited with George Dangerfield *Henry Adams' History of the United States*. His articles in the field of Afro-American history include: "Why Study Afro-American History?" in William G. Shade and Roy C. Herrenkohl, eds., *Seven on Black* (1969); and "The Economic and Racial Components of Jim Crow," in Nathan I. Huggins, et al., *Key Issues in the Afro-American Experience* (1971). Professor Scruggs is presently at work on a major study of Alexander Crummell.

## OKON EDET UYA

Okon Edet Uya is a professor of History at Howard University. He received the Bachelor of Arts degree from the University of Ibadan in 1966; the Master of Arts degree in 1968, and the Doctor of Philosophy degree in 1969, both from the University of Wisconsin.

Professor Uya is the author of three books: *From Slavery to Public Service: Robert Smalls, 1839-1915* (1971); *Black Brotherhood: Afro-Americans and Africa* (1971); *Black Civilizations: A Cultural History of Black People in Africa and the New World,* coauthor with John Willis and Tony Morrison (1973). He has written many articles on African and American history.

## RAYFORD W. LOGAN

Rayford W. Logan was born on January 7, 1897, in Washington, D.C. After completing M Street High School in 1913, he was graduated Phi Beta Kappa from Williams College in 1917. Enlisting in the United States Army in 1917, he was promoted to first lieutenant of the 372nd Regiment of Infantry in January 1918. He served at the front in the Argonne Forest and in Camp Ancona, near Bordeaux, until his discharge in August 1919.

During his expatriation in Europe from 1919 to 1924, he was secretary and interpreter at the 1921 Paris session of the Second Pan-African Congress and at the Third Pan-African Congress in London in 1923; and he was deputy secretary of the Pan-African Association in Paris from 1921 to 1924. From 1925 to 1930 Professor Logan taught history, other social sciences, and foreign languages at Virginia Union University. In 1929 he received the Master of Arts degree in history from Williams College. After completing his residency in the Graduate School of Arts and Sciences, Harvard University, he served from

1932 to 1933 as assistant to Dr. Carter G. Woodson, editor of the *Journal of Negro History*. In 1932 he received the Master of Arts degree and in 1936 the Doctor of Philosophy degree in history from Harvard. From 1933 to 1938 he was head of the department of history at Atlanta University.

In 1938 Professor Logan joined the faculty of the department of history at Howard University, where he was head of the department from 1942 to 1964. Appointed Professor Emeritus of History in 1965, he served as historian of the university until 1969. During his tenure at Howard, Professor Logan taught European history, Latin American history, Negro history, African history, and United States history. While he was head of the department, the graduate program was strengthened and broadened, culminating in the university's approval of a doctorate program in history in 1962. He was reappointed professor on February 1, 1971.

Dr. Logan's investigation of conditions in Haiti contributed to the withdrawal of the United States Marines in 1934. In August 1941 the government of Haiti conferred upon him the National Order of Honor and Merit with the rank of *Commandeur,* "in recognition of the high esteem of the government of the republic." From 1941 to 1942 he was a member of the Advisory Committee of the Coordinator of Inter-American Affairs. At that time he made an on-site study of agrarian problems in Cuba, Haiti, and the Dominican Republic. Dr. Logan was from 1940 to 1945 chairman of the Committee on the Participation of Negroes in National Defense. In 1945 he was an accredited correspondent for the *Pittsburgh Courier* at the San Francisco Conference which organized the United Nations. He served as a member of the United States National Commission for UNESCO from 1947 to 1950. Following the death of Dr. Woodson, he was director of the Association of the Study of Negro Life and History and editor of the *Journal of Negro History* and *The Negro History Bulletin* from 1950 to 1951. He was an accredited nongovernment observer for the NAACP at the 1951 Sixth General Assembly of the United Nations in Paris. During

1951 and 1952 Professor Logan was a Fulbright Research Fellow in Paris, studying the administration of the French overseas and trust territories. His foreign travels included tours of Curaçao, Aruba, West Africa, and northern Europe. In 1960 he attended the Eleventh International Congress of Historical Sciences in Stockholm. In addition to his teaching and writing, Dr. Logan has lectured widely in the United States and abroad. In recognition of his distinguished contributions to historical scholarship and public affairs, Williams College conferred upon Professor Logan an honorary Doctor of Humane Letters degree in 1965.


# JOHN W. BLASSINGAME

John W. Blassingame is an outstanding young historian. He began his higher education at Fort Valley State College, where, in 1960, he earned his Bachelor of Arts degree. The following year he received the Master of Arts degree in history from Howard University. In 1971 he received the Doctor of Philosophy degree from Yale University.

In recognition of his scholarship, he was awarded a Faculty Research Grant by Howard University in 1962; an Esso Faculty Fellowship, 1965-1966; and a Ford Foundation Faculty Fellowship 1969-1970.

Dr. Blassingame served as associate editor of the Curriculum Project in American History at Carnegie Mellon University in 1965. He has taught at Howard University, Maryland University, and Yale University.

Professor Blassingame has published eleven articles. He edited *New Perspectives on Black Studies* (1971); coedited *In Search of America* (1972); and with Louis Harlan coedited *The Autobiographical Writings of Booker T. Washington.*

# BENJAMIN A. QUARLES

Benjamin A. Quarles was born in Boston, Massachusetts, where he received his elementary and secondary education. In 1931 he earned the Bachelor of Arts degree from Shaw University in Raleigh, North Carolina. He received the Doctor of Philosophy degree in 1940 from the University of Wisconsin.

In recognition of his scholarship, he has been awarded fellowships by the Social Science Research Council, the University of Wisconsin, the American Council of Learned Societies, and the John Simon Guggenheim Foundation.

Before assuming his present professorship at Morgan State College, Dr. Quarles served as professor of history and dean of instruction at Dillard University. A leading scholar of Negro history, he has written the following books: *Frederick Douglass* (1948); *The Negro in the Civil War* (1953); *The Negro in the American Revolution* (1961); *Lincoln and the Negro* (1962); *The Negro in the Making of America* (1964); *Black Abolitionists* (1969) and with Leslie Fishel coauthored *The Black American: A Documentary History* (1970).

Professor Quarles is a member of the editorial board of the *Journal of Negro History*. He has been appointed recently as an Honorary Consultant in American History for the Library of Congress and Chairman of the Maryland Commission on Negro History and Culture.

# Bibliography

## Chapter II

Adam, Karl, *The Christ of Faith*. New York, 1957.

Athanasius, *Select Writings and Letters*. Vol. IV, Second Series, of *A Select Library of Nicene and Post-Nicene Fathers of the Christian Church*, edited by Archibald Robertson. New York, 1903.

Ayer, Joseph Cullen, ed., *A Source Book for Ancient Church History: From the Apostolic Age to the Close of the Conciliar Period*. New York, 1939.

Aymro Wondmagegnehu and Joachim Motovu, eds., *The Ethiopian Orthodox Church*. Addis Ababa, 1970.

Barry, Colman J., ed., *From Pentecost to the Protestant Revolt*. Vol. I of *Readings in Church History*. Westminster, Maryland, 1966.

Brightman, F. E., ed., *Liturgies: Eastern and Western*. Vol. I, Oxford, 1965.

Brown, Clifton, "The Ethiopian Orthodox Church," *Negro History Bulletin* (January 1972), pp. 10-11.

Budge, E. A. Wallis, *History of Ethiopia, Nubia, and Abyssinia: According to the Hieroglyphic Inscriptions of Egypt & Nubia & Ethiopian Chronicles*. Vol. I. Oosterhout N.B., The Netherlands, 1966.

————, ed. and trans., *The Queen of Sheba and Her Only Son Menyelek*, translation from Bezold's edition of the Ethiopic text. London, 1932.

*The Church of Ethiopia: A Panorama of History and Spiritual Life*. Addis Ababa, 1970.

Cosmas, *Christian Topography*, Translated and edited by J. W. McCrindle. London, 1897.

Cowley, R. W., "The Ethiopian Church and the Council of Chalcedon," *Sobornost* (Summer 1970), pp. 33-38.

Daniélou, Jean, and Henri Marrou, *The First Six Hundred Years*.

191

192    AFRICA AND THE AFRO-AMERICAN EXPERIENCE

Vol. I of *The Christian Centuries,* translated by Vincent Cronin. New York, 1964.
Doresse, Jean, *Ethiopia,* translated from the French by Elsa Coult. London and New York, 1959.
Ephraim, Isaac, *The Ethiopian Church.* Boston, 1968.
————, "Social Structure of the Ethiopian Church," *Ethiopian Observer* (1971), pp. 240-88.
Wright, Stephen and Jaeger, Otto A., *Ethiopia: Illuminated Manuscripts.* New York, 1961.
*The Fetha Nagast (The Legislation of the Kings),* translated from the Geez by Abba Paulos Tzadua and edited by Peter L. Strauss. Addis Ababa, 1968.
Eusebius (Pamphili), *Ecclesiastica historiae libri decem, ejusdem de vita Constantini IV nec non Constantini oratio ad sanctos et panegyricus Eusebii,* Edited by Ernest Zimmerman. Frankfurt, Germany: In Libraria Hermanniana, 1822.
Haberland, E., "Christian Ethiopia," in Roland Oliver, ed., *The Middle Age of African History.* New York, 1967, pp. 7-12.
Hammerschmidt, Ernst, "Jewish Elements in the Cult of the Ethiopian Church," *Journal of Ethiopian Studies* (July 1965), pp. 1-12.
Heyer, Frederich, "The Teaching of Tergum in the Ethiopian Orthodox Church." Vol. II of *Proceedings of the Third International Conference of Ethiopian Studies.* Addis Ababa, 1966, pp. 140-50.
Hippolytus, "Heads of the Canons of Abulides or Hippolytus, Which are Used by the Aethiopian Christians." Vol. V of *Ante-Nicene Fathers Down to A.D. 325.* Grand Rapids, Michigan, 1952, pp. 256-57.
Hughes, Philip, *The Church in Crisis: A History of the General Councils, 325-1870.* New York, 1964.
Huntingford, G. W. B., trans. and ed., *The Glorious Victories of Amda Seyon: King of Ethiopia.* Oxford, 1965.
Jesman, Czeslaw, *The Ethiopian Paradox.* London, 1963.
Jones, A. H. M. and Elizabeth Monroe, *A History of Ethiopia.* London, 1955.
Jungman, Josê A., translated by Francis A. Brunner. *Early Liturgy to the Time of Gregory the Great.* Notre Dame, 1959.
Kihl, Melvin J., *Ethiopia—Treasure House of Africa: A Review of Ethiopian Currency and Related History.* Santa Monica, California, 1969.

Lulseged Lemma, "Ethiopia: An Interpretative Essay," *Negro History Bulletin* (January 1972), pp. 6-8.

Mara, Yolande, *The Church of Ethiopia: The National Church in the Making*. Asmara, Ethiopia, 1972.

Mercer, Samuel A. B., *Ethiopic Liturgy: Its Sources, Development, and Present Form*. New York, 1970.

Moore, Dale H., "Christianity in Ethiopia," *Church History* (September 1936), pp. 271-84.

Moscati, S., *Ancient Semitic Civilization*. London, 1957.

Pankhurst, Richard. *An Introduction to the Economic History of Ethiopia from Early Times to 1800*. London, 1961.

————, *State and Land in Ethiopian History*. Addis Ababa, 1966.

Phillips, Wendell, *Qataban and Sheba: Exploring the Ancient Kingdoms on the Biblical Spice Routes of Arabia*. New York, 1955.

Revised Constitution of Ethiopia. *Negarit Gazeta*, November 4, 1955.

Saxena, Nawal K., *Ethiopia Through the Ages*. Calcutta, India, 1968.

Schaff, Philip, ed., *The Creeds of the Greek and Latin Churches*. Vol. II of *The Creeds of Christendom with History and Critical Notes*. New York, 1890.

Selassie, Sergew Hable, "Church and State in the Aksumite Period." Vol. I of *Proceedings of the Third International Conference of Ethiopian Studies*. Addis Ababa, 1966, pp. 5-8.

*The Seven Ecumenical Councils*. Vol. XIV, Second Series, of *A Select Library of Nicene and Post-Nicene Fathers of the Christian Church*, edited by Philip Schaff and Henry Wace. New York, 1900.

Socrates, *The Ecclesiastical History: Comprising a History of the Church, in Seven Books, From the Accession of Constantine, A.D. 305, to the Thirty-eighth Year of Theodosius II, Including a Period of 140 Years*. London, 1892.

Sozomen, *The Ecclesiastical History: Comprising a History of the Church, from A.D. 324 to A.D. 440: Also the Ecclesiastical History of Philostorgius as Epitomised by Photius, Patriarch of Constantinople*, translated by Edward Walford. London, 1853.

Taddesse Tamrat, "A Short Note on the Traditions of Pagan Resistance to the Ethiopian Church (14th and 15th Centuries)," *Journal of Ethiopian Studies* (January 1972), pp. 137-50.

Theodoret and Evagrius, *A History of the Church, From A.D. 322 to the Death of Theodore of Mopsuesta, A.D. 427, and From A.D. 431 to A.D. 594*. London, 1854.

(Abba) Tito Lepisa, "The Three Modes and the Signs in the Ethiopian Liturgy." Vol. II of *Proceedings of the Third International Conference of Ethiopian Studies.* Addis Ababa, 1966, pp. 162-87.

Ullendorff, Edward, "Candace (Acts viii 27) and the Queen of Sheba," *New Testament Studies* (1955-56), pp. 53-56.

————, *Ethiopia and the Bible.* New York, 1965.

————, *The Ethiopians.* London, 1960.

————, "Hebraic-Jewish Elements in Abyssinian (Monophysite) Christianity," *Journal of Semitic Studies* (July 1956), pp. 216-56.

Walsh, Martin de Porres, *The Ancient Black Christians.* San Francisco, 1969.

## Chapter IV

Bennett, Lerone, Jr., "The Making of Black America: Part IV," *Ebony* (October 1970), pp. 46 ff.

————, "The Making of Black America: Part V," *Ebony* (November 1970), pp. 56 ff.

Bennett, Robert A., Jr., "Black Episcopalian: A History from the Colonial Period to the Present," in *Encyclopedia of Black America,* edited by Virgil Cliff and W. A. Low. New York, forthcoming.

Block, Muriel L., "Beriah Green, The Reformer." Master's thesis, Syracuse University, 1935.

Bracey, John H.; Meier, August; and Rudwick, Elliott, eds., *Black Nationalism in America.* Indianapolis, 1970.

Bragg, George F., *History of the Afro-American Group of the Episcopal Church.* Baltimore, 1922.

Brotz, Howard, ed., *Negro Social and Political Thought 1850-1920: Representative Texts.* New York, 1966.

Cromwell, John W., *The Negro in American History.* Washington, 1914.

Crummell, Alexander, "The Acquisitive Principle Among Negroes," *The Southern Workman* (October 1898), pp. 196-97.

————, "Address at Evening Prayer," *The Southern Workman* (April 1896), pp. 71-72.

————, *Africa and America.* Springfield, Mass., 1891.

————, "The Attitude of the American Mind Toward the Negro Intellect," The American Negro Academy, *Occasional Paper* No. 3. Washington, 1898.

————, "Charitable Institutions in Colored Churches." December 5, 1892.

————, "Civilization, the Primal need of the Race," The American Negro Academy, *Occasional Paper* No. 3. Washington, 1898.

————, "Founder's Day Address," *The Southern Workman* (March 1896), pp. 46-49.

————, *The Future of Africa.* New York, 1862.

————, *The Greatness of Christ.* New York, 1882.

————,"Remarks," *The Anti-Slavery Reporter* (June 25, 1851), pp. 87-89.

————, "1844-1894: The Shades and the Lights of a 50 Years' Ministry."

————, "The Solution of Problems the Duty and the Destiny of Man." 1895.

Curtin, Philip D., *The Image of Africa: British Ideas & Action.* Madison, 1964.

Du Bois, W. E. B., *The Souls of Black Folk,* in *Three Negro Classics.* New York, 1965.

Factor, Robert L., *The Black Response to America: Men, Ideals & Organization from Frederick Douglass to the NAACP.* Reading, Mass., 1970.

Ferris, William H., *The African Abroad.* 2 vols. New Haven, 1913.

————, "Alexander Crummell, Negro Apostle of Culture," The American Negro Academy, *Occasional Paper* No. 20. Washington, 1920.

Fox, Ronald N., "The Rev. Alexander Crummell: An Apostle of Black Culture." B.S.T. thesis, General Theological Seminary, 1969.

George, Carol, "Richard Allen and the Rise of the Independent Black Church Movement, 1788-1837." Ph.D. dissertation, Syracuse University, 1970.

Green, Constance McLaughlin, *Secret City: A History of Race Relations in the Nation's Capital.* Princeton, 1967.

Harding, Vincent, "W. E. B. Du Bois and the Black Messianic Vision," *Freedomways,* IX (Winter 1969), pp. 44-58.

Lynch, Hollis R., *Edward Wilmot Blyden: Pan-Negro Patriot, 1832-1912.* London, 1967.

Meier, August, *Negro Thought in America 1880-1915: Racial Ideologies in the Age of Booker T. Washington.* Ann Arbor, 1964.

Moses, Wilson J., "The Evolution of Black National-Socialist Thought: A Study of W. E. B. Du Bois," in *Topics in Afro-American Studies,* edited by Henry J. Richards. Buffalo, 1971, pp. 77-99.

Okoye, Felix, "The Afro-American and Africa," in *Topics in Afro-American Studies,* edited by Henry J. Richards. Buffalo, 1971, pp. 37-58.

Phillips, Henry L., and Anderson, Matthew, "In Memoriam of the Late Rev. Alexander Crummell." Philadelphia, 1899.

Redkey, Edwin S., "The Meaning of Africa to Afro-Americans, 1890-1914" (manuscript).

Wahle, Kathleen O., "Alexander Crummell: Black Evangelist and Pan-Negro Nationalist." *Phylon* XXIX (Winter 1968), pp. 388-395.

Walker, Orris George, Jr., "The Episcopal Church and the Negro." B.S.T. thesis, General Theological Seminary, 1968.

# Index

Abba Afse, 51
Abba Aragawi, 51
Abba Pentalewon, 51
Abolition of slavery, 103-105, 115, 138, 151
Abun, 41, 43-45, 47
Aelurus, Timothy, 50
Africa, artifacts from, 76; geography of, 3-4, 7-15, 68; history of, 7-10, 15-27, 29-32; nationalism, 28; natural resources, 10-15, 107, 109; stereotypes of, 28-29
African Free Schools of New York City, 78
African independence, 60
African studies program, 3-32
Afrikaners, 97-136
Afrikaner Bond, 113
Agar-Hamilton, J. A. L., 103
Agaw, 38
Alexander, 35-36, 40
Alexandria (Egypt), 36, 43, 50, 52
Almuqah, 37-38
Alwah, 24
A. M. E. Review, 139
American Colonization Society, 78
American Communist Party, 142-143, 146-147

American Dilemma, by Gunnar Myrdal, 140
American Historical Association, 147
American League of Colored Laborers, 139
American Missionary Association, 130
American Negro Academy, 80, 84, 89, 91
Amharic, 23
Andover Theological Seminary, 78
Anglo-Boer War, 108-110, 113
Angola, 74
Antislavery Conference of the European Powers, 69
Anulinus, 35
Apartheid, 97-136
Aptheker, Herbert, ed., Autobiography of W. E. B. Du Bois, 143-144
Aquezat, 37
Arabia, 39
Arabic, 24
Ares. See Mahrem.
Arianism, 36, 45, 50
Arius, 35-36, 45-46
Arles, synod, 46
Arthur, Chester, 67
Arwe, 38

197